For Sarah

Who knows as no other how we use language to give meaning to things.

BIS Publishers
Building Het Sieraad Postjesweg 1
1057 DT Amsterdam
The Netherlands
T (31) 020 515 02 30
bis@bispublishers.com
www.bispublishers.com

ISBN: 978 90 6369 432 6

Art direction: Bart van Esch
Layout: Bart van Esch
Final editing: Robin Straatman

Made possible by:
Fontys Academy for Creative Industries, Tilburg

B/SPUBLISHERS

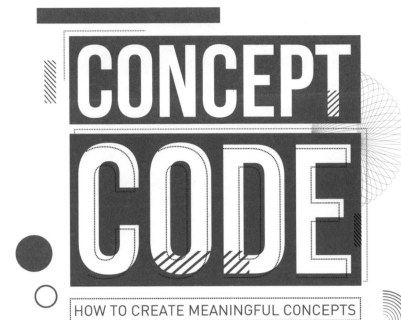

CONCEPT CODE

HOW TO CREATE MEANINGFUL CONCEPTS

BIS

TABLE OF CONTENTS

CHAPTER 3: CONCEPT THINKING

CHAPTER 4: DEVELOPMENT, THE DORMANT CONCEPT

TABLE OF CONTENTS

CHAPTER 5: FRAMING, THE AWAKENING CONCEPT

CHAPTER 6: ACTIVATION, THE LIVING CONCEPT

CHAPTER 7: TOOLS, SOME OPTIONS

PREFACE

We live in a world so full of information that instead of having troubles finding information resources, we are now faced with the challenge of actually cancelling out unwanted data. Instead of going to a pond to find knowledge, we now have a huge, fierce river that's growing faster, wider, and stronger every day. Presently, we consume as much information in one day as people did in a whole lifetime a hundred years ago. We cannot absorb all the content available on a subject of our interest, because there's simply too much of it being published. A sender of a message has to come up with new ways of breaking through the noise in order to reach its receiver. This is where concepts come in. Conceptual Thinking takes on the challenge of explaining this in a fascinating and eye-opening way.

In the creative industry we commonly use terms such as 'thinking outside the box' or 'stepping outside your comfort zone'. To us this represents a natural process of coming up with new ideas and concepts. The actual innovation lies in the process of thinking sideways, or in any way that you normally wouldn't. This approach combined with reality and logic creates solutions. At Snask, we have always sailed west when the industry leaders told everyone to sail east, up when they said down, etc. Not to go against the grain, but to form our own opinions, processes, and structures. Our own way of doing things, without being influenced too much by conservative or non-modern methods and ways of working. We are not alone in doing so. There are so many with the same mindset and approach around the globe. What we all have in common is a way of thinking that makes everything possible.

By doing things our way, we realise that we can do almost anything we want. We create bar concepts. We open restaurants. We invite our friends to self-organised athletic events. We connect with each other on creative meetups and conferences. The possibilities are endless with this new way of seeing yourself and your abilities as a creative. We believe that creativity is not something you can be taught, but that it is something we are all born with. Gradually, we are taught how not to use it in service of becoming something called a grown-up instead. Luckily, we believe that everyone can still go back and tap into that creativity and curiosity that was always there. By using our creativity and creating concepts, we are not only able to create our own brands, but also to help other brands and sectors in society. Creative people have successfully remodelled what unemployment solutions look like, how elderly people connect with each other, how a map can be used in modern society, how we can spread information much simpler and faster, etc. The list goes on and keeps growing as you read this.

Using concepts and lateral thinking is the way to come up with new ideas and keep up with an ever-changing society. For us at Snask, it's the only way forward and we use it every day. We teach it, we feel it, we breathe it. And what makes it so damn satisfying is that we are far from alone in doing so. One day, this way of thinking will become obsolete, but that's the way it should be.

The same goes for design; the step the follows ideas, the process that translates a concept to visual form. Design can solve problems that a concept can only highlight. At Snask, we firmly believe you need a concept for every design, and every concept needs a visual form. It follows that they are very much intertwined and inherent in everything we do. A good example of the importance of design is offered by a recent project of ours, which is a concept that turns any dirty puddle into clean, drinkable water with the use of sunlight. The design is a divided tank that you fill with water and place in the sun, which allows the intense rays to destroy the bacteria. After twenty minutes, you close it again and are left with a tank full of drinkable water. The container also has a very clearly illustrated instruction manual on how to do this, without any written text, so that anyone can use it no matter their language or literacy. This is an example in which concept and a design work beautifully together and create something very meaningful.

More and more people are starting to realise that creating concepts and designs is part of natural human behaviour and something that anyone can do. You will find many inspiring stories in this book and perhaps even learn a few things. But remember: don't just look at the pretty pictures!

/Fredrik Öst
Founder and creative director at SNASK

INTRODUCTION

Both of us are teachers at the Fontys Academy for Creative Industries in Tilburg. Six years ago, we were preoccupied with developing lessons for our concepting course. We were looking for good examples from the creative industry to illustrate the principle of concepting that was emerging at the time. We were particularly looking at vision – which we now describe as the dormant concept of organisations – but it quickly became apparent that this was hard to find. We then tried to pinpoint visions on the basis of the products/ services offered (living concept) from the organisational concept. We mostly did this on intuition, feeling, but we did not have any evidence to share with our students. In the meantime, several books had been published, but we were still looking for suitable examples from the field and a method that responded to the needs of our students in order to make the subject of concepting less 'vague'. Apparently, this has not yet been done before. After days of frustration, Gaby tweeted the following on 12 December 2010 on her twitter account: "Sanne and I have a new dream; writing a book! All that litera-ture on concepts and visions; it is time for a new book!" That very same week a publisher contacted us, asking us how serious this dream of ours really was. That is how our story started, and how we ended up writing the Dutch book Conceptdenken, van slapend naar levend [Concept thinking, from dormant to living], published in 2013.

WHY THIS BOOK?

After the book had come out, we soon received questions from students and the business sector on how to get from one stage to the next. How do you ensure coherence? How do you translate the dormant concept into the living concept? This presented a huge obstacle for students. What is the connecting factor between these three stages? And how can you apply these to the principle of concept thinking? This question intrigued us to such an extent that we took it as our starting point for working on this new book. We discuss the question of how the stages of concept thinking are connected and how you can apply that connection in the concept development process. We started exploring, travelled across the world, spoke with experts, and listened to national and international success stories in order to be able to give the subject of concept development a boost. At this moment, the creative industry is one of the top nine sectors in the Dutch economy for which the government wishes to excel internationally. The Human Capital Agenda for the top sector of the creative industry states that internationalisation for the creative industry is a must, not merely an option. Thus, the creative industry will increasingly be operating internationally. This requires knowledge of international development among creative professionals. We were able to take a look behind the scenes at interesting concept brands such as Rapha and FREITAG. We have spoken with progressive designers in the USA and have seen and understood that in some ways they have a different working method than here in Europe.

WHAT ARE THE LIMITATIONS OF THIS BOOK?

This book assumes an international perspective. Of course, 'an international perspective' is a broadly interpretable term. Therefore, it is desirable to define a clear scope. This scope also defines the limitation of the research. We have opted for an international, western perspective. As a consequence, the limitation is that a large and important international part of the creative industry, for instance in Asia, is not covered in this book.

In this book we limit ourselves to concepts that generate meaning with a focus on creating symbolic value. That does not mean that the functionality of concepts, and by extension their functional value, does not play a role, but we simply do not exclusively focus on functionality. Rather, we see this as a form of (product) innovation.

In this book, we cover the (important) role of design within the stages of a concept, but wish to emphasise that this is not a book primarily for designers. The knowledge and tools we offer help you as a concept developer in optimising your design choices and thus in strengthening your concept, but this does not make it a design book.

Nor is this in any way a scientific book, although we have taken an investigative approach. We have interviewed various experts in the broad field of concept thinking. We want to share our knowledge and insights, add depth to the method of concept thinking, and introduce the readers to the social developments they are also part of, whether or not they like it.

Finally, this book takes on the definition as formulated in the previously published book *Conceptdenken, van slapend naar levend* [Concept thinking, from dormant to living]. A possible limitation is that the international definitions of a concept will not always correspond to each other. This has been taken into account as much as possible in the interviews and the incorporation of them.

THIS BOOK IS FOR

The book is designed in such a way that it does the creative industry justice, making it a must-have for inspiration for students, teachers, and people interested in concepts/concept development alike. Thus, this has been written for multiple target groups. The most important target group is students following a course in a field within the creative industry. In our opinion, this is not restricted to students of communication and/or creative subjects, but also appropriate for the more economically oriented courses. Every part of the concept needs to be just right: one plus one must at least equal three, and preferably more. The Concept Code is more. In addition to concept thinking, the emphasis is on 'concept action': the execution of the concept. After all, concepts are not just creative in nature, but will also have to be implemented and activated. This means that you also need to consider the feasibility and the effects: what value do you create with the concept and what type of business model can be used for this? Entrepreneurship and creativity go hand in hand. We hope to offer students more in-depth insight into the already existing methodology and some more support for properly executing the living concept.

In addition, the book will also be valuable for any professional interested in concepts and concept development. We hope that anyone who feels connected to the wonderful field called concept thinking will enjoy reading this book and getting inspiration for bringing concept thinking and concept action into practice.

CONTEXT

CONTEXT

· ·

The world is constantly changing. Fast-track shifts are occurring left, right and centre. People increasingly long for meaning and depth, but also want the product or service they select to function according to their needs and expectations. Because people differ so much from each other, the value that a concept adds can be different for each individual. The emergence of the Internet has opened up a huge number of possibilities. The data that consumers leave behind regarding their behaviour on the Internet offer a new image of human behaviour, which has become accessible to companies. What occurs internally in companies is, in turn, increasingly more visible to the larger public. In order to gain the trust of the consumer, it is necessary to be transparent and this has ushered in the 'age of transparency'. In addition, we are becoming increasingly aware that visuals have a stronger appeal to people than words to. This influences how companies develop their concepts. This chapter discusses the important shifts in the global mindset that have resulted in the increasing expansion of the creative industry. We will also take a look at the importance of concept thinking within the creative industry and why this way of thinking is necessary in our changing world. Furthermore, the way in which consumers and products move in this context will also be explored. Moreover, we zoom in on the importance of the creative industry and the manner in which concept thinking fits into this.

In doing so, it must be noted that the creative industry mainly focuses on innovation by means of crossovers between various sectors. This book looks beyond merely conceptual crossovers.

1.1 'SUPPOSED TO' IS A THING OF THE PAST

In the past, your birth announcement card also served as your ID. You would follow into your father's footsteps, become a baker and go to the same church as your parents because your social environment would require that of you. The society expected you to adhere to the correct standards and values, and ensured that there was a certain degree of participation in the social community. Reflecting on your own identity was not necessary: your opinions and individuality were formed by the local social environment you were a part of. That was simply how things were supposed to be. You would not act from a personal drive – there was always some form of 'supposed to' involved.

Important social developments in the twentieth century have freed individuals from this 'supposed to'. Employees have become more independent and social class and ideology no longer determine who is part of your social circle. For instance, you personally choose whether or not you go to church and which one you join. In some European countries, societies have been liberated from domination and dictatorship. You decide for yourself how you construct your identity based on the values instilled in you during your upbringing. The increased access to entertainment, affordable services and products, and the seemingly endless digital environment have made us less dependent on our direct social surroundings. Nowadays, you become a baker because you love organic products and wish to run a socially responsible business. You do yoga twice per week because it makes you feel so wonderfully Zen. Then you drink a tasty cup of Nespresso, because you value quality. You leave your small-town birthplace to move to New York, Rome or Sydney.

In our current society, nothing in set in stone: you are the director of your life, the maker of your identity. That has brought our society to a turning point. Tomorrow looks different from today. We see much more than we used to, as many things have become more transparent due to the emergence of digital media. The world has therefore opened up more. As a result, it has become increasingly evident that our banks are failing and we no longer wish to be dragged into the abyss. In response to this, various social concepts are emerging. These are concepts that, in addition to economic value, also create social value. Within these concepts, consumers are increasingly coming together and self-organising. A good example of this is the Dutch broodfonds (literally meaning bread fund). This is a collective of entrepreneurs who organise their own safety net. If an entrepreneur falls ill, they temporarily have no income. Therefore, this is a risk they will want to sufficiently take care of. With a 'bread fund' entrepreneurs support each other on a voluntary and equal basis. The system was created by and for entrepreneurs, who know what their own needs are. They make clear agreements and are transparent for everyone; bread funds are based on trust. A bread fund consists of at least twenty and a maximum of fifty entrepreneurs, who set aside a monthly amount on their personal bread fund account. This initiative demonstrates how groups of people unite around needs, partly from a motivation to turn a profit, but also with the wish to be able to contribute to their personal values: independence and responsibility.

The world, which used to mainly be ruled from a rational perspective and logistical processes, is rapidly changing. 'We cannot solve our problems with the same thinking we used when we created them,' according to Albert Einstein. Daniel H. Pink describes this in his book *A whole new mind* as follows: 'Left-brain-style thinking used to be the driver and right-brain-style the passenger. Now, R-Directed thinking is suddenly grabbing the wheel, stepping on the gas, and determining where we're going and how we'll get there.' The previously underappreciated right brain with all its emotions, creativity, and intuition has now taken centre stage and is at least as important as the analytical left brain. The two brain hemispheres need each other in order to progress.

We will have to bounce back and forth between both hemispheres and seek a balance between the two. Logic and emotion will increasingly need to collaborate as one powerful machine. The creative industry in particular is a sector in which these two brain hemispheres come together. Before we dive deeper into the shifts that offer the basis for this growing industry, the following sections offer our perspective on the creative industry.

1.2 THE CREATIVE INDUSTRY

Before we get to our definition of the creative industry, we first want to take you on a journey through the evolution of the term 'creative industry' and the corresponding perceptions. The terms creative economy, cultural industry, and creative industry are regularly used interchangeably, but is this justifiable? The term 'creative economy' was launched briefly after the turn of the century in order to indicate a new phase after the Industrial Age. This term builds on what was previously introduced as knowledge economy (De Voldere & Rutten, 2008). In this context, the main objective is to design and come up with creative and smart solutions, resulting in products and services

Figure 1.1 Cocentric Circels Model

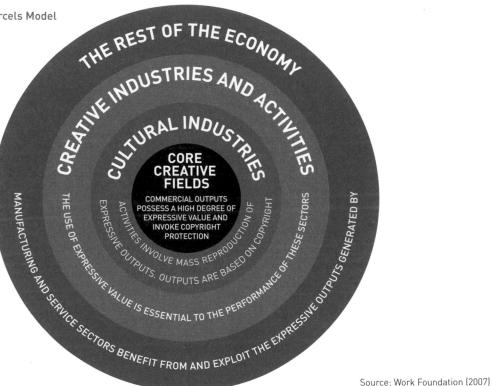

THE REST OF THE ECONOMY

CREATIVE INDUSTRIES AND ACTIVITIES

CULTURAL INDUSTRIES

CORE CREATIVE FIELDS

COMMERCIAL OUTPUTS POSSESS A HIGH DEGREE OF EXPRESSIVE VALUE AND INVOKE COPYRIGHT PROTECTION

ACTIVITIES INVOLVE MASS REPRODUCTION OF EXPRESSIVE OUTPUTS. OUTPUTS ARE BASED ON COPYRIGHT

THE USE OF EXPRESSIVE VALUE IS ESSENTIAL TO THE PERFORMANCE OF THESE SECTORS

MANUFACTURING AND SERVICE SECTORS BENEFIT FROM AND EXPLOIT THE EXPRESSIVE OUTPUTS GENERATED BY

Source: Work Foundation (2007)

with an added value that respond to the experience of consumers. These solutions also have the objective of making an increasingly more significant contribution to the greater social challenges we face globally. In 2001, the creative economy gained attention through the British writer and media manager John Howkins. He made a distinction between various domains and labelled selected domains 'creative' that had never before been considered part of the creative industry. That immediately brings us to the next term: culture industry.

Since the eighties, the core of the cultural industry has been characterised by a symbolic or expressive element. In those days, the heart of the cultural industry was globally represented by UNESCO, the UN organisation for education, science, culture and communication. This encompassed a wide range of domains, such as music, art, fashion, design, media, film, television, and radio, etc. All these fields are characterised by a significant economic value, but also by a social and cultural significance. The term 'creative industry' was coined for much broader productive manifestations.

The origin of the discussion on the creative industry can be traced back to the United Kingdom, where the Department for Culture, Media and Sports (DCMS) developed the following definition: 'Those activities which have their origin in individual creativity, skill and talent, and which have a potential for wealth and job creation through the generation and exploitation of intellectual property.' (DCMS, 1998)

In the model (figure 1.1) of The Work Foundation you can see how these terms relate to each other. The model is based on the concentric circles model by Throsby (2001). The model differentiates between the cultural and the creative industry, but they are both placed within the perspective of the overall economy. This model demonstrates that the heart of the activities within the creative economy is based on expressive values. It represents the purely creative content. This content is created by an author, painter, dancer, or for instance filmmaker. The commercialisation of these purely expressive values takes place in the cultural industry. For example with music, television, and radio. The next circle represents the creative industry, which in addition to expressive values also adds a functional value. The model demonstrates that the creative industry builds on that which results from the cultural industry. The activities of the creative industry are directly meant for end users.

Statistics Netherlands – the central Dutch governmental institution responsible for gathering, processing, and publishing statistics for the benefit of government, science, and business – applies the following subdivision in their limited definition of the creative industry:

1. MEDIA AND ENTERTAINMENT

Typical components of this subsector are the radio and television industry, the film industry, the music industry, the book publishing sector, and the gaming industry.

2. ARTS AND CULTURAL HERITAGE

This subsector is primarily concerned with aesthetic expression. This category of arts applies to practitioners of the performing arts, but also institutions such as theatres, concert venues, and museums.

3. CREATIVE BUSINESS SERVICES

This concerns creative services for business clients. Belonging to this category are e.g. advertisements, communication, and various forms of design.

The foregoing subdivision demonstrates that the creative industry is chopped into pieces. The question that follows is then where the boundaries are exactly. Does the advertising agency that creates a new campaign for a museum belong in the category of arts and cultural heritage or creative business services? In some countries the advertising agency would in this case not even be considered part of the creative industry, but rather the cultural industry. This is due to the distinction that is made between creative business sectors directly focused on end users (creative industry) and creative business sectors supplying to other companies (cultural industry). In other words: is it the end user, the designer/the activity, or the business division that provides the starting point for determining

>>THE CREATIVE INDUSTRY IS NOT LIKE THE BOUNDARIES BETWEEN DIFFERENT AREAS, NOT REALLY STRICT. THAT MEANS THAT EVERYONE BRINGS THEIR OWN INFLUENCE AND INSPIRATIONS AND SO THEY CAN CREATE A BIG MIX.<< Malika Fauvre

whether something ought to be considered part of the creative industry? For our present purposes, it is more useful not to take the subdivision in business sectors as a starting point, but the core activity of the creative industry: creating symbolic value. In the context of this core activity, we distinguish between the development, the framing, and the activation of symbolic value. The type of activity thus determines whether it can be categorised as part of the creative industry. In doing so, we distance ourselves from the discussion on the subdivision in terms of business sector.

1.2.1 ASPECTS OF THE CREATIVE INDUSTRY

In order to arrive at a demarcation of the creative industry, we will first discuss the common denominators we discovered during our exploration of the various definitions and models around the creative industry. What shows up in most definitions, for instance in those by UNCTAD (United Nations Conference on Trade and Development) and the European Commission, is that in addition to economic value, symbolic value is also created. This is the entrepreneurial part of the creative industry, which knows how to convert creativity into business. At the very least, this offers

an interesting perspective for connecting creativity to entrepreneurship. There is a remarkable paradox at play here. Creativity and commercial logic do not always go well together. The term creative industry offers hope for creative entrepreneurship on the one hand, while on the other hand it is evident that entrepreneurship within the creative industry still leaves something to be desired from an economic perspective. This is due to an unfamiliarity with entrepreneurship within the industry, for instance due to a lack of knowledge of business models and earnings models within this and other sectors. You need to be able to practice entrepreneurship in order to sell mostly immaterial value.

Practicing entrepreneurship in the creative industry means that you need to be able to be commercial, but also keep an eye on the social component (Stevens in van Vliet & Wijkhuis, 2015). Another key term that kept recurring in our research is collaboration. Being creative is a first step towards a different approach to social issues, but if you are then unable to map out any application or distribution, you will still not arrive at any solutions. For that reason, many interdisciplinary methods have emerged in the creative industry for which collaboration between the left and right brain hemisphere is necessary. In comparison to other disciplines, the creative industry distinguishes itself in terms of mindset. A different mindset is at the core of creativity: it allows a creative professional to offer a major contribution to the creative industry. 'We will never be able to outsource creativity to a machine; it comes from people. That is the power of the creative industry,' according to Arjan van den Born, professor of creative entrepreneurship (van den Born in van Vliet & Wijkhuis, 2015). Human creativity is the most important driver of the sector. This might lead one to believe that consensus on what activities belong to the creative industry should easily be reached. After all, the professionals responsible for the creation process will then virtually all belong to the creative industry. We find this a bit too simplistic, but it does offer points of departure for us to work with. The creative industry produces meaningful products and/or services that are the result of creativity and entrepreneurship. The creative professionals are active in professions characterised by the development, production, and implementation of symbolic material and the representation of reality. The most important differentiating and recurring feature of the creative industry is the dominant role of meaning in products and services.

Products and services are purchased due to their content and symbolism (van der Giessen et al, 2015). Another evidently recurring element is that the creative industry possesses the ability to help other sectors increase their added value. If you zoom in on this even further, you might say that only the business sectors delivering to other companies fall under the creative industry. However, that is contradictory to what section 1.2.1 describes. Here, the creative industry was actually shown to focus on end users. That is another reason why the creative industry cannot be demarcated on the basis of a domain or business sector, but rather by looking at the keys of the creative industry. So far, we can say that the creative industry is characterised by:

CREATIVITY

ENTREPRENEURSHIP

CREATION OF SYMBOLIC VALUE

CROSS-DISCIPLINARY COLLABORATION

KNOWLEDGE

1.2.2 PERSPECTIVE ON THE CREATIVE INDUSTRY

We have looked into the common denominators and recurrent characteristics within various theories, models, and definitions of the creative industry. It remains a diffuse concept, which begs the question: does the creative industry exist as such? And if so, what does it include exactly? At the moment of writing this, there is much commotion around the concept of the creative industry. For instance, the creative industry is growing exponentially in the Netherlands and its surrounding countries, and is offering an increasingly significant contribution to the (Dutch) economy. The creative industry is currently one of top nine sectors of the Dutch economy in which the cabinet wishes to excel internationally. This generates much attention for the creative industry, but surprisingly enough there is no generally accepted definition of the term. Or rather, we have not been able to find this definition so far. Entrepreneurs, governments, designers, and others involved all formulate their own definition. The recently published book *We moeten eens koffie drinken* [Let's grab a coffee sometime] by Van Vliet & Wijkhuis (2015) confirms this. They claim that the creative industry is an industrial mindset, an umbrella term, a form of recognition, or even an austerity measure. That lack of clarity surprised them and they started to explore the term of creative industry by comparing various views. Everyone determines their own framework and within that context there are no correct or incorrect definitions, according to them. This makes sense to us. In order to better place the principle of concept thinking within the creative industry, we gladly offer our own definition in order to prevent any further confusion. In doing so, we also determine our own framework in this book. Similar to the definition of 'concept', it is also virtually impossible to give the 'creative industry' one single definition. There are simply too many definitions in circulation. The creative industry produces meaningful products or services that are the result of creativity and entrepreneurship. It is our opinion that it is important to understand that you need to offer added (symbolic) value to consumers and organisations in society. Considered from that standpoint, you are not creating your own ideal product or service, but a meaningful solution to which creating symbolic value is vital. For arriving at our classification of the creative industry, we took the European definition of creative industry as a point of departure: 'The creative industry is a sector that, in addition to economic value, also creates and exploits symbolic value. It rests on the ability of individuals, groups, companies, and organisations to

create meaning'. We take the activity as stated in the definition as a starting point for categorising or not categorising something as belonging to the creative industry, for which we replace the activities of 'creating' and 'exploiting' to those of 'developing' and 'framing', respectively. In addition, we add the activity of 'activating'. The creation of symbolic value is then the result of developing, framing, and activating creative, meaningful content and design. In this way, we can largely reach consensus on what activities belong to the creative industry. We maintain that professionals and organisations directly responsible for the development of the concept are virtually always part of the creative industry. This makes the business sectors involved in the activation of the developed concepts, such as concert venues, broadcasting companies, and museums, part of the creative industry as well. All these companies are often in dialogue with the makers/developers about the eventual form of the products and content of the expressions. They are responsible for access to the creative content and as such have an influence on the symbolic value. For instance, the activities of the gaming sector also fall under the creative industry. In this case, we are not referring to the development of software, but the content, the story, and the interaction between the player and the game typical of gaming. In determining whether an organisation does or does not fall inside the scope of the creative industry, it is therefore important to never lose sight of the essential activities: the development, framing, and activation of symbolic value. There are various organisational connections to be recognised between the various activities. The manner in which the content is developed, framed, and activated can entirely occur in-house. However, in the case of for instance creative

THE CORE ACTIVITY OF THE CREATIVE INDUSTRY IS CREATING SYMBOLIC VALUE.

CREATING SYMBOLIC VALUE
=
DEVELOPMENT
+ FRAMING
+ ACTIVATION OF THE SYMBOLIC VALUE

business services it is commonly about the creation of meaningful content for other business sectors. In that way, creative business services providers deliver creative input to several business sectors. They strengthen the distinctive capacity of companies and their products and services and can be of value for each activity. Another organisational form within the creative industry emerges when an organisation develops independent creative content, commercialised and therefore activated by the other business sectors. In addition to symbolic value, the creative industry also offers functional value. A design from an architect will have aesthetic value, but must also be functional in use. Keeping the aforementioned in mind, we have made a classification for the creative industry connected to our definition and phasing of a concept, subdivided into the dormant, awakening, and living concept. The three activities together create and communicate meaning and ensure a meaningful experience for the consumer.

DORMANT CONCEPT

All activities for which the development of creative, meaningful content and design is essential. These are focused on the symbolic value and the development of the vision.

AWAKENING CONCEPT

At this stage the abstract philosophy from the dormant concept is provided with further meaning by connecting language to it. Language in word and image.

LIVING CONCEPT

Implementing and activating symbolic and functional material, in physical and virtual form.

Now that we have a better handle on the concept of the creative industry and our own classification, it is time to start looking at which shifts form the base of this growing industry.

1.3 THE WORLD IS CHANGING

As a society, we need to accept that a transformation has taken place in the past decades. We live in a time of social and economic transition. Various international shifts influence our mindset and thereby the principle of concept thinking. They influence society as it is today. Some shifts are noticeable and contribute to a continually growing creative industry. These are also important for where we are now:

FROM OR-OR TO AND-AND: FUNCTIONAL AND EMOTIONAL NEEDS

FROM FAÇADE TO TRANSPARENCY

FROM TRANSACTION TO RELATION

FROM WORDS TO VISUALS

FROM OWNING TO SHARING

FROM FINANCIAL PROFIT TO MULTIPLE VALUE CREATION

1.3.1 FROM OR-OR TO AND-AND: FUNCTIONAL AND EMOTIONAL NEEDS

For a long time, organisations were the centre of focus, creating values around their products and services. However, consumers have been the focal point for a while now: organisations need to respond to what consumers want. This shift from organisation-focused to consumer-focused is not new, but the needs of the consumer have significantly changed in the past years and that is something organisations need to take into account. Consumers no longer want any ready-made packages, but organisations that contribute to attributing meaning to their living and user environment.

Supply-driven marketing used to fulfil the material needs in the nineteenth century. In the meantime, applying new knowledge to improve the material needs is no longer sufficient for worldwide competition.

Nowadays, these types of needs have already been fulfilled, and emotional needs are becoming increasingly important. It is increasingly about the power to develop new services and products quicker and more effectively. In particular, it is about designing and creating opportunities and solutions that result in services and/or products with significant added value and aligned with the experience of consumers. Therefore, a shift has taken place from a product and material economy to an experience economy. Subsequently, it had shifted on to an economy of meaning, in which experience and the meaning of the product or service is the main focus. The creative industry contributes to this by creating symbolic value in addition to economic value. What does the product or service stand for? Do I consider this meaning important? What value do I attach to this? Does it make sense? For instance, does it contribute to a successful confrontation of the major social challenges our current society is faced with? People want to organise the economy of meaning in a useful manner. Consumers want authenticity, small-scale, simplicity and/or exclusivity, but many experiences are too superficial and too commercial to them. They look for intensive, personal, and memorable experiences that enrich their lives and give it meaning. In any case, daily life may never become boring or mundane.

Various trends reflect this small-scale and exclusive focus. An example of this is the moving store concept: shops that suddenly pop up in a big city and then disappear again just as suddenly. If you buy something in such a shop, you truly own something exclusive. In addition to this need for an individual experience, the collective experience is also playing an increasingly bigger role; being together with others adds an extra dimension to experiences. For instance, events such as festivals, demonstrations, and football games. The collective experience itself is not the result of coming together, but coming together is the basis that ensures that the experience itself becomes more intensive.

Moreover, in addition to meaning – and thus the symbolic aspect – functionality becomes possible again. This is because products can once again distinguish themselves in terms of function due to technological developments. That renders the perception of performance by the consumer important again. After all, ultimately a product or service will still simply have to fulfil a functional value for the consumer. If the functionality is optimised within the scope of technology, that can yield a competitive edge through the application of creativity. Organisations would do well to then consider the needs of the consumers instead of the demand. The demand often refers to a product or service, but what need underlies those? As a producer, you therefore need to ask yourself the question: What need will I be fulfilling? For instance, a visitor to the website of Funda – the Dutch leading online media company in the area of real estate – is looking to find a new house. The emotional need that might underlie this is that the consumer wants a happier future. In our current society, producers need to be acutely aware of the fact that consumers wish to see both their emotional and functional needs fulfilled. This shift from or-or to and-and has accelerated in the past years, partly due to technological progress. In many cases, the creative industry makes use of new technological developments. The relation between the creative industry and technology can be traced back to the central role of language and information in both domains.

1.3.2 FROM FAÇADE TO TRANSPARENCY

It is increasingly visible to the larger public what goes on in organisations. The chance to pose as something you are not has become a thing of the past. In a digital

> **>>TO GET FANS YOU HAVE TO BE VISIBLE AND TRANSPARENT.<<** Fredrik Öst, SNASK

society, transparency is highly relevant: if organisations are not open themselves, others will ensure insight into their affairs by means of critical reviews, for instance. In addition, authorities have lost their authority. In our current society, an organisation without regard has no value. Trust is a key term here. Consumers want to know whom they are dealing with and just fulfilling your promise no longer suffices. People want stories and they want to know what place the organisation takes up in society. Trust is no longer a right, but needs to be earned by organisations. You need to say what you do and then actually do it. It is not so much about what you communicate, but about showing who you are in your behaviour. The Internet has made the world more transparent. If someone wants to know anything about you, Google will let them know who you are. You as an organisation no longer determine who you are or wish to be; it is now up to consumers to decide what you are. The boundary between external and internal communication has increasingly blurred due to this development: what goes on in companies is also visible to the larger public. Moreover, social media has made the age of transparency even more of a reality. The receiver has hereby also become the sender.

Trust is something you can earn by being transparent to all stakeholders of your organisation. These are all the parties that can influence or be influenced by the organisation. For instance, consumers, employees, shareholders, partners, interest organisations, politics and press. These stakeholders have mutual relations and these can also influence the image of the organisation. It is important to be authentic and credible. As an organisation you need to prove yourself and primarily reflect your promise in your behaviour. In order to earn trust and understanding you need to engage in a dialogue with your stakeholders. In doing so, you ensure that the sharing of information will simply snowball.

1.3.3 FROM TRANSACTION TO RELATION

The age of transparency has led to a collective shift from transaction to relation. This means that the focus has increasingly shifted to the human. As mentioned in the foregoing, earning trust has become increasingly important for organisations and social interaction with the consumer is key in this. Trust is a basic principle. The more ways organisations can find to open up, the more trust they build with consumers. It is important that organisations collaborate with consumers, in which it is vital that the organisation truly listens and looks at what the consumer does and has to say. This requires openness. The organisation looks for connection with the consumer, which grows increasingly important during their customer journey (the 'journey' the consumer takes before he or she purchases a product). To this end, the organisation needs to communicate a relevant message at every moment, so that the consumer remains enthusiastic. This relevant message must match the interests and focus of the consumers at that time. For instance, fewer and fewer statistical interfaces are created. Interfaces will increasingly be able to respond to the moment. The information displayed depends on the situation of the carrier. For example, your physical behaviour is linked to your personal digital cloud. An example of such an interface is Disney's MagicBand, a bracelet that replaces the entrance ticket. It is a new payment method on the basis of the use by and, by extension, the behaviour of the user. Organisations no longer consider the consumer exclusively as a buyer, but as someone with whom they wish to build, maintain, and deepen a relationship. The value a concept adds can be different for each consumer. This makes it evident that we are increasingly transitioning from a rational thinking to a human-focused paradigm. That human-centred paradigm implies a softer approach to humans and organisations on the way to long-term relations.

The perception of the consumer determines the quality of his or her sense of involvement in the entire customer journey. As an organisation you need to know what value you add at what moment. This is partly determined by the consumer's social experience of the concept. The social experience consists of the manner in which someone identifies with the concept (personalisation) and the interaction he or she experiences with the concept. Therefore, do not only listen to the consumers, but also look at their behaviour. In principle, everything an organisation does or does not do leaves an impression, effectively communicating on a continual basis. Communication is a two-way stream, which has recently increased in significance due to social media. Communication of a strong brand not only explicitly conveys a message, but also implicitly communicates the identity of the organisation.

As an organisation, you need to seek out the customer and work on a solid relationship. Ensure that you have something in common with the consumer. Not until this relationship has been established, will the consumer start talking about your organisation to other consumers, and that is what you want!

1.3.4 FROM WORDS TO VISUALS

People do not always behave rationally. Consumers mainly make decisions regarding purchases on the basis of emotions. In doing so, cognitive dissonance often occurs. In the event of cognitive dissonance, an uneasy feeling emerges when something we believe or hope for is contradicted by the facts, when our behaviour is not in line with the picture we have in our minds, or when we have two different ideas that are mutually exclusive. According to research, people feel a strong urge to reduce that dissonance by adjusting or rationalising their views or behaviour. Let us consider an example in order to clarify this phenomenon. You have determined in advance what expectations your

>>LOGIC GETS YOU FROM A TO B.
IMAGINATION GETS YOU EVERYWHERE.<<

Albert Einstein

favourite holiday destination should meet. All holidays you consider will be assessed on the basis of aspects you consider important. The price of the flight ticket, the location of the hotel near the sea, and the closest village, for example. Through Zoover or Booking.com you assess all the aspects you value by means of the reviews and scores. Rationally speaking, you would of course opt for the holiday destination with the highest review score. However, you still spend time deliberating the pros and cons on the couch at night until you end up with the exact trip you had apparently already decided on beforehand.

From this example you can conclude that the producer needs to attach greater value to the behaviour of the consumer than to what the consumer says. Consumer research regularly falls short because organisations are not aware of the ideas of the consumer at a conscious and unconscious level. It is often assumed that consumers think in a rational, linear manner and that behaviour can be explained along those lines. The idea that consumers can be 'fed' a message, and that this message then actually sticks, is outdated. We now know that unconscious thoughts and feelings are the actual drivers of customer behaviour.

Due to these new insights, producers need a change in mindset. They need to start basing their choices on the mindset of the consumers. The earlier example of the holiday choice demonstrates that our actions contain very little logic. According to Gerard Zaltman, author of the book *How Customers Think*, no less than 95 per cent of our opinions and thoughts are determined in our subconscious. As mentioned, conscious thought processes purely serve to rationalise our behaviour. Therefore, it is highly important to investigate and explore the entire iceberg, including what lies under-neath the water surface (the emotionality), as emotion and reason work together.

Another important fact is that thoughts are based on images rather than on words. As soon as consumers talk about products or services in a metaphorical and thus visual manner, unconscious thoughts more easily make it to the conscious level. Because the consumer can now picture the images, deeper lying associations can also rise to the surface more easily. An image can contain many associations and connections, which ultimately supports a better memory. Zaltman offers the sidenote to this that the brain, the world of thought, the body and society are interconnected and cannot be investigated separately from each other.

VISUAL LANGUAGE

The fact that the thoughts of the consumer are based on images is interesting. It also explains our increasingly important visual culture. Images pass us by every day from early morning till late in the evening. Images as a communication medium have a powerful effect and play an increasingly significant role in communicative situations. The visual culture has existed for years, but due to the technological possibilities its impact is rapidly increasing. Nowadays, everyone can easily visualise and share his or her life story. Every mobile telephone has a good photo and video camera and editing these images can also be done in the blink of an eye. Therefore, it is increasingly easier to use images in addition to text in order to convey your story. This emerging trend is called visual storytelling. The use of visuals in communication will only increase due to the development of for instance augmented reality and diminished reality, FaceTime, Qwiki, and much more. As communication gets increasingly visual, the more traditional forms of communication are also becoming less dominant.

Visuals add meaning to the world in which we live, and we give meaning to the visuals. Visual language is not just the catalyst for this process, but at the same time a powerful form of expression for sharing meanings. For instance, you can use visual language to enforce what you mean, convince or stimulate people, prove or compare things, convey a universal message and provide insight into complex matters. Chapter 5 discusses how you can apply this tool.

1.3.5 FROM OWNING TO SHARING

Boundaries are blurring and the world has become one connected whole due to the arrival of social media. It has become increasingly tricky to determine and demarcate target groups. Once organised by socio-political barriers, society has now been integrated on all fronts. For instance, digital seamlessly transitions into physical, consumer into producer, and biology into technology. The lifting of socio-political barriers was followed by globalisation and individualisation. Producers often used to have knowledge of one truth and with that knowledge they would know how to market a certain product or service. Back in the day, that was still possible because the society was less complex and the needs of the various layers were much closer together. Nowadays, everyone has something to say and everyone considers themselves an everything expert. Predominantly due to the developments in the field of the Internet, a network economy has emerged. The creative industry is the perfect example of this strongly growing network economy. Consumers can find anything they want to know on the Internet. Moreover, due to mobile Internet, this information is always available at your fingertips. If you want to know what the weather will be in South Africa the day after tomorrow, you simply look it up right away. Together, we are constructing new information, and by extension knowledge, which we can then share with the rest of the world. YouTube is a good example of this. It is not for nothing that 'Broadcast yourself' is their promise. Nowadays, everyone can make their own video and post it online. Thus it is very easy to share your knowledge, learn from each other, and gain access to various kinds of information. People increasingly move in a so-called horizontal network, right through everything, and no longer let themselves be steered from one central point. The consumer becomes the producer of a product or service on the net. He or she is the so-called prosumer: producer and consumer at the same time. The classic hierarchal relationship no longer exists and producer and consumer are increasingly operating on equal grounds. We make our own truth and personally choose who we are and where we belong. The possibilities are unprecedented. This behaviour fits in with the social movements that we see around us: from vertical to horizontal, from central to decentralised. Due to the emergence of the network society we personally have influence on our sense of meaning and are increasingly able to define it for ourselves. We want customisation and we want to adjust products to our own taste and style. We wonder what is relevant for us and what party fits in with that. We make a choice and then enter into dialogue with the organisation in question. This dialogue forms the foundation for personalised value creation. The consumer together with the organisation adds meaning to the product or the service. This creates a win-win situation for the individual consumer, the organisation, and the other consumers. In our current society it is expected of you that you think for yourself. The post-modern individualist has become a DIYer: like a child that makes a collage, they cut out everything they consider valuable and craft something new out of those pieces. That is how they create their own perfect world. Consumers no longer follow, they lead. One person can start a small company that could grow into a large production company serving a worldwide market. Due to rapidly increasing connectivity, coordination between various parties has become easier. Because boundaries are blurring and everyone is connected, you can easily make use of someone else's knowledge, distribution centre, or factory. Access has become more important than owning. This signifies a shift from possession to use. Our attachment to material prosperity is decreasing. Nowadays, it is primarily about the services, the functions that the products fulfil. Instead of having a car, is more important to have the opportunity to get from A to B at the time you need to. A good example of this is Car2go. Car2go is very simple: reserve, get in, drive, and park. There is always a Car2go in the vicinity. The door can simply be opened with the Car2go application. It is fun, inexpensive, and you contribute to helping the environment. At this moment, the system can already be used in big cities such as Amsterdam, Berlin, Hamburg, Vienna, and Rome.

Another example of a concept focused on sharing is Strava. This is a community that consists of athletes from all across the world. Strava is both a community and a web shop that sells products related to running and cycling. Strava assumes that you strive to excel and, in doing so, unleash your potential. With Strava you are never on your own. It is important to be socially sportive, or in other words: share sports performances with each other. This sharing can be done by means of connecting

through mobile devices. This way, participants can motivate and challenge each other. Strava helps consumers log their running sessions and rides, so that they can track and analyse their performances. Strava gives you a little push so that you stay motivated. You can follow friends, join clubs, found your own clubs, and find the best running routes. Moreover, you can track whether your bicycle needs maintenance and what state your running shoes are in. In addition to the free version, you can also create a premium account, which offers even more features. Examples of these are special heart rate zone checks, capacity analysis, and access to special events. The community supports the brand with many positive actions. The brand is held in increasingly high regard by the consumers and as a result gets much free publicity. From this example it is evident that it is important for brands to concern themselves with the passions and interests of their target groups. That way, consumers will start to form a group around your brand. The Internet is a great tool for this, because it allows you to connect people all over the world to your brand and concept. Partly due to the rise of social media, boundaries have blurred. This has paved the way for a network society, with 'togetherness' as its starting point.

1.3.6 FROM FINANCIAL PROFIT TO MULTIPLE VALUE CREATION

In our current society, profit is no longer exclusively expressed in money. Nor is money any longer the norm as a central medium. Instead, we see more and more social concepts emerge in which other 'currencies' can also be exchanged. Entrepreneurship and creativity are the two most important common denominators of the creative industry. One cannot exist without the other, although so far they seem hard to reconcile. In the development of new concepts you keep one eye on creativity and the other on money and the market. You consciously build a concept, using creativity in adding value to new products and services with which money is earned. The social challenges such as an aging population, climate change, security, and renewable energy can make a contribution to sustainable solutions by means of creative entrepreneurship. Generating financial profit is not the first priority in this. In other conceivable situations generating profit could certainly be a first priority, but even here the aim would be to generate multiple value in order to stand out in the market. Business service plays a major role in this. Professionals within this sector create value by positioning the organisation and companies in a specific manner.

1.4 IMPORTANCE OF THE CREATIVE INDUSTRY

In the expanding creative industry shifts in mindset are increasingly evident. Now that you have an idea of the creative industry and these shifts, you will be better able to understand what the importance of the creative industry is. We have already discussed a number of shifts that have made us freer as individuals in the twentieth century and released us from a society divided by socio-political barriers. The danger that lies in this is that societies lose their identities. A society without a shared identity, without shared values and a vision for its future, is much less able to offer solutions to the problems it faces. For instance, consider themes such as food, energy, the environment, health care, and social security. The political realm is increasingly losing its credibility now that the consequences of the economic crisis are becoming noticeable. Most people might not believe in destructive politics, but the lack of constructive ideas increasingly drives people into the arms of conservative and sometimes radical political parties. Although these movements rarely have any constructive or sustainable ideas, they can simply wait for the next economic or social crisis to happen in order to gain votes. A good example of this is the incredible influx of refugees to Europe in the second half of 2015. Progressive parties are often insufficiently capable of converting their concern into a shared goal that connects. The western world needs a shared identity, in which civil engagement is necessary for innovative ideas for building a prosperous and sustainable society. Such social challenges, also known as grand societal challenges, require a crossover mentality. It is in the interest of producers and service providers to achieve sustainable concepts that help us as a society to deal with our challenges. The search for multiple value creation in the post-industrial age has placed us on the track of the creative industry. The creative industry is uniquely suitable to fulfil an exemplary role in this and feature as an initiator. Creative talents make connections between words and visuals, between design and storytelling, and look beyond their own circle. By making smart combinations, they take care of new concepts, products, and services.

The importance of the creative industry has increased in the past years due to stormy developments in information and communication technology. In the meantime, the creative industry is one of the top sectors in the Netherlands, and in these top sectors government, knowledge institutions, and industry meet. The Dutch creative industry aims to become the most creative economy of Europe by 2020. The development, production, and implementation of meaning and the creating of or contributing to experiences form the core of the sector. The heart of the services and products in the creative industry thus consists of the exchange of meanings. The creative industry adds the power of imagination by for instance using prototypes to show that products and services can work differently and better. It is becoming increasingly important to have an innovation-focused mindset in order to offer solutions to the challenges society is faced with. From this growing creative industry, sectors such as agriculture, education, and the healthcare sector are also supported in their need for innovation. The creative industry can help these sectors increase their added value. For instance, they can better position or renew themselves after interference from the creative industry. Walter Amerika, expert in the field of the creative industry in the Netherlands, indicates that these connections can make the world a bit more honest, transparent, beautiful, healthy and cleaner. Thus, much hope has been placed in the creative industry.

1.4.1 CREATIVITY AND THE CREATIVE INDUSTRY

Creative talent that offers shape and content to the value of creativity is deeply rooted in the creative industry. Talented people make connections between words and visuals, between design and storytelling, and look beyond their own circle. By making smart combinations, they produce new concepts, products, and services. The fact that this results in creativity playing a major role within the creative industry is thus evident. The initial attention resulted from the work of Richard Florida's *Rise of the creative class* (2002). In the meantime, the importance of the creative talent for the creative industry, and to a certain extent also for the entire economy, has been underlined. The creative class, as Richard describes it, is therefore a much broader group. The category of creative professionals as we identify them for the creative industry, is characterised by the development of symbolic material and the visualisation of (giving life to) it. The actual role of creativity within the industry is not always clear-cut. Creativity is a broad concept. It can refer to finding original applications, to another way of looking, or to developing artistic expressions. It can also refer to so-called l'art pour l'art. The importance of creativity in our current society is certainly being expressed in the growing creative industry. In particular, it is about the competencies and skills applied by creative talent for the benefit of creating symbolic value within the creative industry (Rutten, 2014). If the functionality of a concept is optimised within the scope of technology, that can yield a competitive edge by means of the application of creativity. Creativity needs to be imbedded in the organisation to fulfil all activities belonging to the creation of symbolic value. In this book we deal with concepts that contain an element of symbolic value. These typically come with copyrights or other intellectual property rights.

1.5 WHY CONCEPT THINKING?

Now that you know within which playing fields concepts are important, you will surely understand that concept thinking contributes to the creative industry. It is a way of thinking that is aligned with the core activities and features of the creative industry. Concepts connect

various loose elements, make complex matters simpler, and ensure that these complex matters receive and give meaning. Especially making connections is becoming increasingly important – for instance due to globalisation – and this leads to the emergence of connecting creativity: everyone and everything is interconnected. The human is a meaning-making machine, wanting to arrive at understanding. The urge to explain things is inherent in humans. We want to make sense out of nonsense. Nothing humans make can therefore be without thought and feeling. The age of the new way of thinking has arrived. Earlier on, we already briefly discussed the two brain hemispheres and how they depend on each other. Nowadays, the right brain hemisphere – with its emotion, creativity, visual perception and intuition – receives central focus, whereas the analytical left brain hemisphere used to be considered more important in the past. The right brain is more conscious of the whole and is skilled at making associative connections. Lateral thinking is becoming more important than linear thinking. People no lon-

ger want to understand the world on the basis of loose elements, but from a perception of interconnection. Holistic thinking – which looks at the whole and makes connections – offers the key. Therefore, it is logical that concept thinking is becoming increasingly important in the creative industry. Concept thinking ensures that innovation-focused thinking becomes more sustainable, and thus useful for a longer period. After all, a continual stream of innovation is necessary, as this is the soil for the creative industry. For decades, the focus has been exclusively on financial value, but this is increasingly being demonstrated as an overly one-sided perception. Consumers want to experience the story in every touchpoint with the concept, and so continually be fed. In doing so, the producer must meet the emotional and functional needs of the consumer. Every part of the concept needs be just right: one plus one must at least equal three, and preferably more. In addition to concept thinking, the emphasis is on 'concept action': the execution of the concept.

VISION,
VALUES
AND CONCEPT

VISION, VALUES AND CONCEPT

In order to explain 'concept thinking', it is first vital to elaborate on the most important terms related to concept thinking. Previous definitions demonstrate that the term 'concept' is not clear, as in our everyday language it is used for a wide variety of things. Sometimes it stands for a rough version of something, but it can also stand for a philosophy or stage leading up to a scientific theory. As a marketing term it stands for coherence between ideas or views. If you look at it that way, everything with coherence is a concept, because behind each object lies a principle, an idea. Think of a cup, a car, a table... After all, you use the object as the maker intended it to be used. A cup does not bring you from A to B and you do not drink your coffee from a car. This book focuses on the definition of concept as a way of thinking, in which differences between ideas or views are summarised at a high level of abstraction. These abstract ideas or views are in turn translated to increasingly concrete levels, in other words: to the awakening concept and the concept carriers.

Imagine you are on your way to Disneyland with your family. Afters hours in the car, you arrive at the park in a cranky mood. A parking clerk checks in with you: 'Are things all right? Have you had a long journey?' After some moaning from you, you are kindly escorted to your parking spot. Disney demands that all their employees place themselves in the shoes of their visitors as much as possible, because if you pay attention to you visitors and receive them hospitably, they will quickly forget all about that long and tiring journey. 'Here you leave today and enter the world of yesterday, tomorrow and fantasy.' Disney strives for a three-dimensional environment in which the guests are immersed in a story and have fun. Disney wants to create a world in which the guests

can physically step into the well-known Disney stories. Each and every day they manifest this vision with their concept. This is apparent from everything the company does, makes, and communicates. Even the frequently asked questions, such as 'Where is the toilet?' and 'What time does the three-hour parade start?' are kindly and patiently answered by the employees. After all, people that wish to have fun leave their 'brain' at home. Employees respond to this. Not only do they tell you what time the parade starts, but also how to get there, and where you can go for a nice bite to eat. 'When you go to the park, there is no horizon, just Disneyland.'

This chapter will focus on the terms 'concept', 'values', and 'vision'. These three terms are an extension of each other and are interdependent. Without strong values, you can have no vision, and without a solid vision, you cannot have a strong concept: the concept will then have no meaning. Moreover, a concept lacks direction when it has no vision, as a vision steers. The values are the markers with which you indicate the direction of your vision. In order to arrive at a thorough understanding of the terms 'vision' and 'concept', we will therefore start by considering the term 'values'. What exactly are values and why are they important?

2.1 WHAT ARE VALUES?

In every society values and standards play a major role in our daily lives. They form the foundation of our society. Values are mental patterns that describe how you perceive the world, your work, humans, or life in general. They are views on what is experienced as desirable or valuable. The bracelet of your great-grandmother, your holidays in America, or just the cheerfulness of your child: in some way they all have a certain value which makes them valuable, but not directly expressed in economic value. Moreover, various kinds of value exist that are sometimes hard to compare. For instance, there are individual values and collective values, hard and soft values. What do we actually value? And is that which we value today, still valuable next year, too? Values indicate what we consider good and valuable in life, but that can make them quite vague. Honesty, respect, loyalty, responsibility, and freedom are all quite abstract values. You might have a different view of what freedom is than your friend or colleague. Therefore, it is extra important to make your values specific, so that it is clear to everyone what you mean with a value such as freedom. Values are also culturally determined. What is valuable in a European company might not be in an American or Chinese organisation. Moreover, everyone

also has a different value hierarchy. One person will consider certain values more important than the next. Values are thus highly personal. The pyramid below demonstrates that values can both be taught and innate and can apply to you personally or to a group. Value is therefore a dynamic and relative phenomenon and is determined contextually. Values can change throughout time and can also be determined individually and socially. Concepts arrive at their complete meaning, and thus value, during interaction with the individual. It is all about the value someone attributes to the concept.

2.2 WHY VALUES ARE IMPORTANT

Due to the shifts as discussed in chapter 1, other values than just economic value are at play. It is not just about making a profit, but increasingly about (jointly) creating

Figure 2.1 Three Levels of Mental Programming

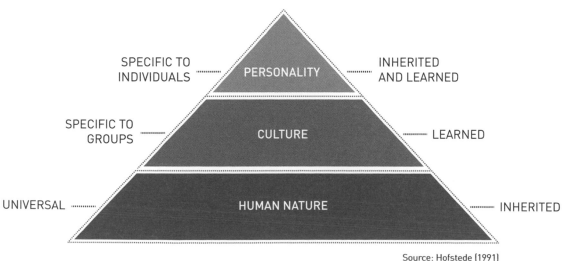

Source: Hofstede (1991)

healthcare and rest, for instance. Instead of organising wealth, it also becoming about organising wellbeing. Organisations make revenue, and thus a profit, which means the economic value is likely to remain important. However, it is the consumers that are prepared to pay money for products or services of an organisation. They do so because it contributes to their personal values, both the functional and the symbolic ones. Organisations can respond to this by also pursuing social values: principles that hold meaning for people as ultimate personal values or as social values. This makes organisations part of the social identity of people. Dr. Paul Rutten, lecturer Creative Business, describes this as a lifestyle value. He refers to the value that consumers attribute to products and services on the basis of elements that appeal to them. They do so because they feel that those elements suit who they are and want to be, which they therefore value, including financially. However, in this perspective 'profit' is not strictly expressed in money, but also in for instance safety, food, time, or happiness. At the start of this book, we already stated that the value a concept adds can differ for each individual, because people are so different. The principle of multiple value creation is evident: the transactions create social, economic, and for instance ecological value at the same time. In other words: from financial profit to multiple (financial, social, and ecological) value, as demonstrated in chapter 1.

2.3 ORGANISATIONAL VALUES VERSUS CONSUMER VALUES

In developing a concept, this book distinguishes between organisational values and consumer values. Consumer values are more directly tailored to consu-

mers. This pertains to the value the organisation adds to products and/or services in the eyes of the consumer (user). Values are also of great importance within an organisation, because they contribute to the vision. Values are necessary for the capacity to formulate a vision. As mentioned, they are signposts indicating how you can add colour to your vision. Values briefly and powerfully indicate 'the way in which an organisation does the things it does'. They add consistency, continuity and eventually credibility to that organisation. We distinguish between internal and external values here. Internal values contribute to the implicit personality of the organisation, the characteristic inner qualities. The external values contribute to the explicit personality. These are the characteristic qualities of the behaviour. In other words: being versus doing. Are you what you say you are? We will apply the concept of 'values' in this book in various ways: the organisational values can be applied as an instrument for positioning and the consumer values as a steering mechanism behind the decision-making process. On the one hand, in concept thinking the (latent) needs of the consumers and users are taken as a starting point. Latent, because these are important needs for the concept developer to respond to. These are those needs that the consumer might not necessarily be able to directly identify, but are definitely present as such. On the other hand, new combinations are sought to arrive at products and services that have not yet been recognised as a need by the consumer, but do fit the organisation. Organisational values work on the basis of the inside-out principle, in which the organisational identity offers the starting point for creation. Consumer values work exactly vice versa, thus outside-in. In this case, creation is approached from the receiver's perspective and his or her values. In concept thinking we do not take on a certain perspective, but a combination of both principles. If you compare the inside-out and outside-in principles with personal interaction, you can ask yourself what would be most pleasant: a person who remains his- or herself in every situation, or someone who adapts to the company he or she is in and therefore has a great sense of empathy? We feel that one cannot exist without the other, just like a concept cannot exist without a vision. The most pleasant people are those who can both listen, remain themselves and act accordingly.

The term consumer values can be subdivided into the economic, functional, emotional, and symbolic value of a concept. In all cases, value is attributed to something, but the unit in which the value is expressed is different in each case. For instance, economic value, or exchange value, if often expressed in monetary terms. Functional value can be expressed in ease of use or user-friend-liness, also called use value. A product or service adds emotional value, for instance if the consumer is crazy about a product or a service due to nostalgia, tradition, or advice from others. In case of symbolic value, the value becomes that bit more intensive; the consumer identifies with an organisation, product, or service. It is about the value that someone eventually attributes to it. Later on in this chapter, it will become clear that concept thinking in any case concerns itself with symbolic values that communicate meaning and are not directly related to the product or service. The central issue is creating symbolic value. But what is that exactly? This calls for a closer investigation of the concept of 'symbolic value'.

2.4 SYMBOLIC VALUE: FROM VALUES TO VALUE

The symbolic value of an experience lies in the capacity of a concept to convey symbolic messages and high-light symbolic meanings. We agree with this revised definition of cultural economist David Throsby (2000). However, this does not make the term operational and therefore measurable. Concepts do not get meaning, and thus value, until interaction with the individual takes place. In that sense, the value is relative and is determined contextually. This will become clearer later on in this chapter.

The symbolic value that an individual attributes to a concept is determined by the symbolic values that underlie it. According to Franzen and van den Berg (2001), you can subdivide your symbolic values into three different categories:

EXPRESSIVE VALUES

These relate to how we want to be seen by others. They are the values that the consumer wishes to display to the outside world, such as wealth. In this case, the signal we send out when we make use of a certain brand is important. Consumers who wear the clothing brand Diesel are independent and Apple users think diffe-rently and innovatively. Rolex owners are professionally successful and Harley Davidson riders have a sense of freedom. The story users are able to tell themsel-ves by means of the brand is becoming more important than the product or the service itself. With expressive values you tell a story to someone else by means of the purchase of a specific product or service.

IMPRESSIVE VALUES

These are focused on our self-perception. They relate to feelings that people personally experience in using a certain product, such as contentment and self-confidence. Impressive values give you a good feeling. One person buys an anti-cellulite cream in order to meet his or her own ideal beauty standard, while the other person goes to a beauty salon in order to achieve the same goal. The content of a value can thus be different for everyone, but the value of 'beauty' is shared. Other examples of impressive values are achievement, wisdom, and care for the family.

ULTIMATE VALUES

These are ideal visions for our personal lives, as we would eventually like to see them shaped. They are the highest values that we wish to live up to and our desired final goals. The expressive and impressive values together form your ultimate values. Examples of

these are inner harmony, a comfortable life, and social recognition.

SOCIAL VALUES

These are ideal representations of the society in which we live and with which we associate the concept, such as a better environment, freedom of speech, and national security.

In the subdivision that Franzen and Van den Berg make, various value forms are hidden. The value a consumer attributes to the concept during the interaction with this concept is determined by the personal values of the consumer. Still, the type of symbolic value can differ. Throsby (2003) proposes a further deconstruction of the concept 'symbolic value' and makes a distinction between ethical value (beauty and harmony), spiritual value (understanding, insight, enlightenment), social value (connection with others, identity perception), historical value (connection with the past), and symbolic

Figuur 2.2 Value Dimensions

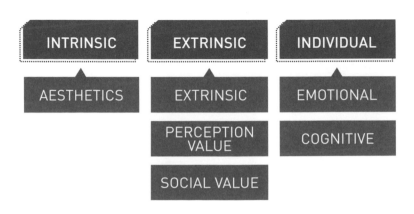

value (carrier of meaning). The subdivision according to Franzen and Van den Berg could be referred to as social value within the deconstruction by Throsby. We have drawn from the deconstruction by Throsby and the research report *Symbolische waarde van creatieven industrieën in Vlaanderen* [Symbolic value of creative industries in Flanders] (Guiette et al, 2011) in order to arrive at our own value diagram. All these dimensions of value within the creative industry can be categorised into the overarching term 'symbolic value'.

INTRINSIC VALUE

The first dimension of the symbolic value can be called intrinsic value. This value cannot be seen as separate from the product. Hereby we can make a subdivision into aesthetic value and historical value. However, in this book we leave the historical value out of consideration. In the domain of heritage it is mainly about the acknowledged historical value and other motives, such as economic value, only come into play in the second place. However, aesthetics is a symbolic value that can be of influence on the functional value of a concept. After all, the way in which something is designed can contribute to the functionality of the concept, which is why we consider this dimension of intrinsic value for concept thinking.

EXTRINSIC VALUE

A second dimension of the symbolic value is formed by the extrinsic value. This is the value that concept developers attribute in advance on the basis of which they develop the concept. People often experience these values immediately and these experiences motivate

them to seek out more of such experiences (McCarthy et al., 2004). These include expressive values as described by Franzen and Van den Berg. Part of this is identity value, in which the concept consciously responds to identity formation of the individual. The identity perception can in come cases transcend the individual, for instance when it concerns a feeling of connectedness with a group. Regarding effects for society it is about social, ecological or economic changes as a result of the concept. This determines the social value of the concept. The experience value lies in the fact that the concept can entertain people and provide fun and relaxation. The type of experience can be different per individual. We further elaborate on this in chapter 3.

INDIVIDUAL VALUE

With these dimensions we refer to the way in which the concepts are valued. This concerns the possible effect, for instance emotion, that the individual can experience from the concept. Examples of this are certain emotions and skills. After all, we already descri-bed in the above that the concept does not get any value until it interacts with an individual, i.e. through the manner in which the individual acknowledges and perceives the experience. It is about the origin of the appreciation that is situated with the individual him- or herself. We make the distinction between emotional and cognitive value. Fun due to knowledge present in the individual ensures a higher cognitive value. An increase in knowledge and skills due to experience can also yield cognitive value, depending on the skills of the individual to develop this knowledge. In other words: how competent are you as an individual to be able to process the concept at a cognitive level? This competence contributes to the individual value of the concept. In chapter 5 and 6 we further elaborate on the way in which you can take a factor such as competence into account in the development of your concept. The emotional value is also a value that each individual will experience differently. What is spectacularly beautiful for one person, can leave another person entirely unmoved.

This demonstrates that people's personal values are important predictors of selection behaviour. The reason for this is that people feel the need for a personal identity in order to have a better understanding of their status and role in life. Therefore, culture and lifestyle play a significant role in the creative industry. The purchase of products and services is an important means for developing the desired identity. Thus values determine our choices and steer our behaviour.

Despite the fact that creating symbolic value is largely leading in the development of a concept, functional values and symbolic values are not separate from each other. Consumers attribute meaning to the concept by means of a combination of both. It is about the relation between these values. The model that offers insight into this is the means-end chain model by Gutman (1982). This model is explained later on in chapter 7. It does need to be said that this model best suits the decision-making process behind functional products.

2.5 VALUE CREATION

Let us circle back to the values in relation to a concept. Creating symbolic value is a prerequisite for the development of a concept. How this value is constructed and what dimensions you as a concept developer include

depends on your starting situation and corresponding strategic choices. The values, and by extension the value the concept will deliver, must be made explicit at the start of the process. In this manner, you create value by making use of the values that lie at the foundation of the strategy of your concept. You can thus say that during the transformation from values to value the value creation is achieved. You thus create (added) value. Creating value is of great importance to organisations, because they derive their raison d'etre from it. The organisational values should not be too general. You will often begin with as many as ten values and ultimately reduce them to a few core values. For instance, banks must all operate with integrity and professionalism, but with good core values alone a bank cannot distinguish itself from the competition. A bank needs to offer meaning and can only do so if there truly is a story behind its values. The core values must be reflected in the behaviour and the attitude of the employees. In addition, they also determine the topics in relation to which the bank communicates and responds, and determine the symbolism the bank uses. The value system and the vision jointly form the basis of the concept. Only in that manner can you arrive at sustainable concepts. The ultimate value is determined by the consumers themselves. They determine whether they appreciate something to a greater or lesser extent, what meaning it has to them, and whether they are prepared to spend money on it. Thus, this indirectly also determines the economic value of the concept. In addition to an exchange value, each object also has a use value (Marx, 1867). The exchange value includes the economic value and the use value indicates the benefits the consumer receives.

Earlier on, we wrote that value creation is increasingly occurring in collaboration. By this we mean that people are increasingly developing from consumers into prosumers; from mere user or receiver to collaborative maker. This movement is facilitated by the network society in which we currently live. We increasingly want to shape values together, but also share these values, and preferably also aim for multiple value creation. Working together, as we were able to see in the foregoing, is typical for the creative industry. A good example of multiple value creation is Schiphol Airport. Schiphol Group describes this as follows: 'To us, "Connecting the Netherlands" means that we continually work to optimise the connection between the Netherlands and the rest of the world. In this way, we hope to contribute to the wealth and wellbeing in the Netherlands and beyond. *Connecting to compete and to complete.*' They develop their activities in a balanced manner, both domestically and abroad. In addition, their core values are the centre of their focus: reliable, efficient, hospitable, inspiring, and sustainable.

2.6 VISION

A vision is a certain attitude, perspective, or motivation regarding a product, humans, or the world. A vision comes from inside the organisation and results from values. Where does your focus lie: inside-out or outside-in? For instance, what social values do you want to respond to? In addition, you can make a conscious, strategic choice to focus on certain dimensions of the symbolic values in combination with the directly observable features that result from functional values. This focus also determines choices later on in the process. The choices that you make are

independent from the starting situation of concept thinking. We dive deeper into this in chapter 3. After making your values transparent, you start determining your vision; that still has nothing to do with what you do, but it does provide a direction to your strategy. The vision is developed behind the scenes; it is an internal story. A vision never contains the terms 'money' and 'profit'; you need to look for actual drives. Of course, money and profit are important for the continuity of the organisation, but they are never the goal in this phase. We implicitly assume that organisations exist to make a profit, which is why economic value is also important. Jeroen Geelhoed (2012) describes the following: 'In that sense money is comparable to the air we breathe in and out. Without air you cannot live, but it is senseless to say that we live to breathe! This does not inspire, it does not connect, and it creates no sustainable value whatsoever.' In order to illustrate the term 'vision', we provide a number of examples. Keep in mind that these are all visions at the highest level of abstraction. We will discuss this in more detail later on in the chapter.

VISION ON A PRODUCT OR SERVICE

Lego feels that toys should stimulate the imagination; you get busy and want to make things yourself.
Google believes that the information of the world should be organised and made accessible for everyone.
FREITAG believes that things and materials deserve a second life. 'We believe in the next life of things.'
Patagonia believes in building the best product, causing no unnecessary harm, using business to inspire, and implementing solutions to the environmental crisis.

CONNECTING THE NETHERLANDS

The Schiphol Group is an airport enterprise with an important social role. The airports of the group, in particular Amsterdam Airport Schiphol, create value for the society and the economy in- and outside the Netherlands.

Connecting the Netherlands is meaningful from multiple perspectives, both from an economic and human standpoint. First and foremost, connections lead to sustainable growth. The more direct connections the Netherlands has with important centres in the world, the easier it is for Dutch companies to trade internationally or attract high-quality information. Connections also contribute to our prosperity. They increase the appeal of Dutch cities as business locations for foreign companies and offices or head quarters; a great good in a globalising world in which economic activities are concentrated in a limited number of metropolitan areas. This is what Schiphol Group calls *'connecting to compete'*. And that leaves the human perspective: *'connecting to complete'*. After all, connections make it possible for people from various countries to meet each other and build social networks. As such, connections contribute to the wellbeing of individuals and societies all over the world.

The network of connections forms the heart of the company. Schiphol has a great number of airlines in its client base. The connections network is carried by their home carrier KLM, both for passengers and cargo. They can only facilitate the connections if they offer the airlines and their passengers excellent infrastructural facilities and offer sufficient capacity. The accessibility of their airports through public transport and by car contributes to their connectivity, both for passengers and for people that work there. The same applies to cargo: a good connection to the railway and road network is essential.

Schiphol Group considers it their task to maintain Schiphol Airport and further develop it as a 'mainport'. The regional airports that collaborate with Schiphol Group – Rotterdam The Hague Airport and Eindhoven Airport – fulfil a crucial role in this. They connect the region with Europe and provide an important complement to the network of Schiphol Airport, both in the field of holiday flights and of business travel. Lelystad Airport will in the future offer space for further development of the mainport function of Schiphol. Moreover, their international participation also contributes to strengthening the mainport.

To Schiphol Group connecting is more than facilitating passengers departing, arriving, and changing planes. They not only develop their airports as points of departure and arrival on a trip, but also as inspiring locations to stay, operate a business, and work. In all their actions they consider their environment. They are highly aware of the impact of the aviation activities on for instance the environment or the spatial consequences. Schiphol takes its responsibility and seeks a healthy balance between the positive and negative effects of its activities. They constantly strive for a conscious consideration of People, Planet and Profit, for instance in their investment decisions, tenders, and other activities.

Source: Schiphol Group, 2015

>>VISION IS A PERSPECTIVE ON THE WORLD, MY VIEW, I SEE THIS.<< Jeroen van Erp, Fabrique

VISION IN HUMANS

Theme park Efteling believes that people should be able to escape their everyday life from time to time. Diesel believes that people determine their own style by mixing and matching their clothes in their own way. Nike believes that if you have a body, you are an athlete. Toys "R" Us believes in putting joy in kids' hearts and a smile on parents' faces.

VISION ON THE WORLD

Starmen feels that you need to do things extraordinarily. If you are not extraordinary, you will not get noticed.
Schiphol believes in Connecting to compete and complete.
TED believes passionately in the power of ideas to change attitudes, lives and – ultimately – the world.
SNASK strives to challenge the industry by doing things differently. They worship unconventional ideas, charming smiles, and real emotions. They see the old conservative world as extremely tedious and as their biggest enemy.
Airbnb is creating a world where you can belong anywhere and where people can live in a place, instead of just travelling to it.

2.6.1 WHY A VISION?

Perhaps you know the story of Alice in Wonderland in which Alice asks the Cheshire Cat for directions: 'Would you tell me, please, which way I ought to go from here?' Alice asks. 'That depends a good deal on where you want to get to,' says the cat. 'I don't much care where,' says Alice. 'Then it doesn't much matter which way you go,' the cat answers (Lewis, 1865).

A concept cannot exist without vision: concept and vision are like brother and sister. In the previous chapter we saw that the consumer is looking for the meaning behind a product or service. He or she not only purchases the product due to the product's properties, but due to the 'why' behind the product or the service. The 'why' is your vision. With a vision you thus answer the 'why' behind the product. It is your raison d'etre. Each concept has its own vision. Without vision it rather constitutes product innovation. We would then consider this the concept carrier of a concept. A vision offers a meaningful framework to the organisation and indicates how it views reality. That framework indicates what an organisation considers important and what it wishes to direct its attention to. It has consciously been compiled and recorded or discussed. In addition, vision provides connection: it connects people by means of common values.

>>THE CLIENTS PURCHASE THE WHY AND THE WHY IS THE VISION.<< Jeroen Geelhoed, Samhoud

>>FORMULATING A VISION HAS HELPED US AND HAS PREVENTED US FROM GOING INTO ALL DIRECTIONS AT ONCE.<< Ronald Ligtenberg, Skyway

Knowing your own vision is essential for lasting success. If you only focus on what you do and not why you do it, you will be faced with a need to change. Without vision your product is the same as that of others' and you cannot distinguish yourself. Organisations with a strong focus on the 'why' are not worried about that; they have a clear vision and on the basis of that vision they make decisions. Because a vision offers direction, it also simplifies decision-making. A vision offers the criteria for assessing activities and behaviour. It is clear that they stand for something. Consumers can agree or disagree, but it always contains some truth, as it is based on objective analysis. You see something happening in your context, within your organisation, in your environment, or with the consumer. A change takes place or you identify a development, a chance or an opportunity – this is an objective fact. As an organisation, you form an opinion about this, which explains the subjective character of your vision. A clear and strong vision cannot be copied. At most, you could copy the visual features of the product or service, but not the soul. In chapter 4 you can find how you develop a vision.

2.7 CONCEPT

After the vision and values comes the concept. The term 'concept' is derived from the Latin word conceptus and was already used in antiquity by philosophers and scientists. Conceptus is the past participle of concipere, the definition of which includes 'develop something in your mind', 'merge' and 'fertilise'. Jan Rijkenberg describes the term 'concept' as a verb: concepting. Concepting is introducing ideas to the market in the form of a brand in order to inspire and motivate consumers.

As you were able to read at the start of the chapter, there are many definitions of the term 'concept'. In addition, the terms 'concept' and 'idea' are often used interchangeably, but a strong concept is much more than an idea. Concepts are a mindset offering direction to concept carriers that ultimately result from it. An idea stands on its own; it still needs to be provided with meaning in order to eventually grow into a concept. A concept is always linked to a vision, and that vision adds meaning.

>>A CONCEPT IS PERHAPS THE FOUNDATION OF YOUR BRAND, YOUR MINDSET.<< Gerben Gerritsen, Rapha

>>A CONCEPT IS A PROMISE THAT CREATES A PREFERENCE.<< Armin David, Starmen

>>YOU CANNOT LABEL IT WITH ONE DEFINITION, THERE IS NOT A MAGIC RECIPE. WHAT IS CONSTANT, THOUGH, IS THAT IT ALWAYS STARTS SOMEWHERE IN THE CONTEXT.<<

Mark de Jong, Kossmann.dejong

>>A CONCEPT IS AN OVERARCHING IDEA BEHIND SOMETHING. IT IS MORE ABOUT WHAT LIES BENEATH THE SURFACE, ABOUT THE NARRATIVE. IT IS FIRST ABOUT WHAT ARE YOU GOING TO TELL, AND THEN FOLLOWS HOW YOU ARE GOING TO TELL IT.<< Malika Favre

>>A CONCEPT IS WHEN YOU GIVE FORM TO CONTENT. I SEE A CONCEPT ON TWO LEVELS: ONE IS THE DESCRIPTION TO BE DELIVERED AND THE SECOND IS MORE THE LOOK AND FEEL.<<

Sarah Drummond

2.7.1 DORMANT, AWAKENING, LIVING

In the book *Conceptdenken, van slapend naar levend* [Concept thinking, from dormant to living] (Crucq & Knitel, 2013) it became clear that there are many definitions of the term 'concept'. After extensive literature review and about forty expert interviews it quickly became apparent that the term 'concept' was not clear. In our everyday language the word concept is used for a wide variety of things. Sometimes it stands for the rough version of something and sometimes it stands for the coherence between ideas and stand-points. Crucq and Knitel (2013) therefore argue in their book that 'concept' cannot be captured by just one definition. As a result, our definition consists of three interdependent stages. International research has resulted in us slightly adjusting the earlier definitions described in our previous book. It does not constitute a complete concept until you have gone through all three stages:

THE DORMANT CONCEPT

As an organisation, formulate an elaborate vision and your core values. Investigate this vision and determine its essence. The dormant concept consists of the essence (core) of the vision, 'the why', and the accompanying core values. The selection of your core values will already determine the direction of your strategy. The dormant concept is developed and communicated internally.

THE AWAKENING CONCEPT

Now that you have translated the essence to paper, you will want to make it visible. To this end, you use a one-liner or notion. Sometimes the essence of your vision is already so strong, that it automatically becomes your slogan, but often you will still have to capture the essence. Language, in terms of both words and visuals, is an important aspect of concept thinking. You need to make sure that your one-liner is well formulated and that it matches your vision. This also applies for your logo and typography. In addition, you need to make the essence of the vision concrete so that the vision can also come alive. You can do so by making the core values tangible. In this process you have to think about how you shape your core values. To this end, the functional values are often applied. In doing this, you further shape your strategy by means of the action plan and think about the type of business model.

THE LIVING CONCEPT

The living concept serves as the sensory evidence of your vision. The concept comes to life by integrating the essence of your vision into all concept carriers you produce. In sum: in everything you say and do. At this stage, the meaning of the concept is actually activated. The concept will start to come alive for all the users, because it can be observed by the senses. The value that the concept adds and the moment at which it does so can differ for each individual, but upon implementation and activation you take the dormant and awakening concept as a point of departure. The plan of action ensures that internally everyone knows how they should bring the vision to life. This is important, because your staff members are the ambassadors of your vision; they breathe it in everything they do. You thus execute your vision by working from the inside out: you start internally with the organisation and as soon as the vision is fully observed here, you can translate the vision and the concept externally in concept carriers. At this stage we make a distinction between implementation and activation. Implementation is focused internally (behind the scenes) and activation is directed to all stakeholders, also referred to as on stage.

A concept without carriers is not a concept – concept carriers carry the concept. If you do not develop the carriers appropriately, the concept amounts to nothing. Without concept carriers the concept still resides in the awakening stage. You make choices for the development of your concept carriers from the dormant and awakening concept. This means that, in addition to functional content, the dormant concept is also provided with meaningful content. After developing concept carriers, we have a living concept. It is not until that stage that consumers, suppliers, or employees get into contact with the concept. They recognise and perceive a concept with its values and vision through its concept carriers. The better the concept carriers have been developed, the stronger the meaningful experience of the concept is.

We can distinguish between various concept carriers. These overlap in some cases, or are present to a greater or lesser degree in the living concept. This depends on the starting situation and the domain within the creative industry in which the activity occurs. When you are only concerned with the activation of the living concept, you will still always have to consult with other business sectors in the creative industry in order to activate the appropriately developed creative content. Which concept carriers do and don't you apply?

We distinguish six concept carriers:

PRODUCT

SERVICE

ORGANISATION

COMMUNICATION

PHYSICAL ENVIRONMENT

NETWORK

In chapter 6 we will further elaborate on the manner in which you can develop the concept carriers by means of content and design, so that it contributes to a meaningful experience for the consumer. From hereinafter, whenever we use the word concept in this book without specific definition, the context must make it clear what stage we are referring to.

FREITAG

Why is FREITAG doing this? What is their motivation? This is where they are unique. Many companies make bags and accessories, thus the 'what' or the living concept. Significantly fewer companies make bags and accessories from used truck tarps and recycled materials, and even fewer do it with the kind of passion FREITAG does. FREITAG is a good example of how you can create, produce, and exploit meaning on the basis of multiple value creation. The core values of FREITAG are symbolic in nature, but are certainly not disconnected from the economic value. FREITAG's extensive vision, which they identify as the WHY, consists of a number of elements they deem important: such as: next life, the founding story with the bicycle bags, liking people, intel-

ligence, added value, inner value, honesty, simplexity, thinking in cycles. FREITAG likes to think things through in such a way that their products and projects last longer. In the beginning, there was the bicycle. Their bags were originally made to carry things on a bike. They used dumped bicycle inner tubes as one of their key materials, and they still do so to this day. FREITAG likes people: their customers are friends, not target groups. They look for gaps in the market relating to modern life and try to find new answers. According to them, intelligence connects design with ecology and humour: sustainable fun. In addition to intelligence, they also stand for culture. This alone creates an ideological added value. Responsibility is an integral part of what they do. FREITAG is mindful of inner value. Their bags are not just brimming with quality and functionality, but

also contain hidden details. These details make people happy and make the selling, owning, and using of the bag a great experience. FREITAG is thoroughly genuine, unique, and authentic. They reduce complexity without becoming trivial. Reduction, dropping the superfluous, and focusing on the essential and the meaningful are always their goal. Finally, the Why also contains thinking in cycles. Waste turns into something sustainable, as they use its material and give it a new life.

THE DORMANT CONCEPT

'FREITAG believes things and materials deserve a second life. We believe in waste and ideas.' This is essentially FREITAG's vision, the 'why' as described above. FREITAG has six core values with which they shape their WHY. These are being honest, slightly fucked up, intelligent, urban, recontextualised, and functionally designed. This identity defines their everyday behaviour, their working behaviour, their design behaviour, and their communication behaviour.

THE AWAKENING CONCEPT

FREITAG has recorded its way of thinking and acting in a booklet that is handed out to every new employee . It is called 'What the F, How and Why'. The booklet lays the foundation for the way in which FREITAG distinguishes and expresses itself. In addition, it is the tool according to which they assess everything they do. Everyone at FREITAG knows what the values are and how they should be implemented.

HONEST: FREITAG is thoroughly genuine, unique, and authentic. This does not just refer to their products, but also refers to the arguments they use to sell the products.

SLIGHTLY FUCKED UP: FREITAG is used, not polished, rough, direct, tough, and unusual. Their belief is that their uniqueness gives them the confidence to get things done in their highly individual manner.

INTELLIGENT: FREITAG keeps the future in mind. They act sustainably and reasonably. At the same time, they pursue innovation with ingenuity and playfulness. Playfulness is a big part of all their products and communication. They allow themselves the luxury of laughter. At themselves and at the challenges of life, in response to which they create products. Their humour is ironic to the point of being self-deprecating, but is never aggressive, hurtful, or fatalistic, sarcastic or cynical.

URBAN: FREITAG was born in the urban environment is produced in the urbs, and is largely sold in the urbs. They are an urban brand and they credibly convey an urban lifestyle.

RECONTEXTUALISED: FREITAG removes objects, materials, thoughts, and services from their usual environ-

ment and puts them in a completely new context, changing their purpose.

FUNCTIONAL DESIGN: FREITAG products and services are distinctive, function fanatic, and always of a very high level of quality.

Part of their strategy is 'no ads'. They promote their products without advertising. They do not advertise, they communicate.

THE LIVING CONCEPT

Things are either completely FREITAG or not at all. There is a clear idea behind the things FREITAG does. They implement their vision and core values in all their concept carriers. This makes FREITAG highly recognisable, always and anywhere. No matter where and when people encounter FREITAG, everything is done to offer them a consistent concept experience. At every touchpoint the values of FREITAG are communicated and lived. They sell their stories, including their personal story. Their products all express their principles. The FREITAG product, made from recycled truck tarps, always remains the central focus. However, FREITAG is more than its bags. The FREITAG gift box is more than reusable packaging. Tonnage, cartonage, repurposing, and ambiguous statements; what they make is never just about the product, they create a holistic design. They invent and sell solutions. Their design is not embellishment. Their design makes sense, and it creates functional and timeless goods. Tarps can protect anything, if they are made functional.

>>WE BELIEVE IN THE NEXT LIFE OF THINGS.<<

2.8 THE CONCEPT LADDER

It can occur that you create a concept within another concept, and within that one perhaps yet another. We call these the layers within concepts. The illustration of the ladder visualises these layers in concepts. At the top of the ladder we find the dormant concept: this is the basis and also the highest level of abstraction. This concerns the mindset that is leading for every choice you subsequently make, based on the symbolic value, whether or not combined with functional value and economic value. The awakening concept is located a little lower on the ladder and adds meaning to the concept, offering more of a grasp of the dormant concept and an appearance. Look at it this way: the lower on the ladder, the closer to the ground. The closer to the ground, the more tangible and thus concrete your concept is. When the concept is already tangible, you

will notice that you will have fewer concept carriers to develop. The higher up the ladder, the more emotional and abstract the concept is, and because the concept is more emotional, there is space for more concept carriers. The more abstract the meaning of the concept, the further it can be stretched to other disciplines or categories. The highest level of concept thinking is free of discipline. Under each concept another concept can in turn be categorised. Whenever you start creating a concept, you always test whether it matches the concept at a higher level on the ladder by asking yourself the question: Is my concept aligned with the essence of the vision of the higher concept? The ladder model in figure 2.3 displays the layers within concepts.

Let us take another example for a moment, that of Rapha, in order to clarify the layers within concepts. Rapha was founded in 2004 and had just one mission:

Figure 2.3 Ladder Model

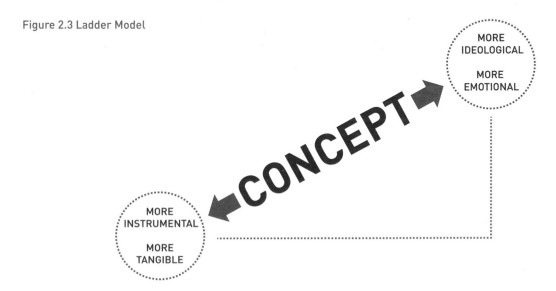

design the very best cycling clothing and accessories in the world. They want to share their passion for the field of competitive cycling. Rapha products are designed without compromise for the most demanding cyclists. Rapha makes use of the best fabrics and components in order to manufacture clothing and accessories that offer cyclists performance, comfort, and style of an unequalled high level. In the beginning it was thus all about real quality clothing. Later on, other concepts and accompanying carriers were added on the basis of that same quality and passion for sharing in the field of cycling. Rapha is thus the brand concept and is located at the top of the ladder. Under this concept you could develop various other concepts. Rapha certainly does this, for instance with Rapha Cycle Clubs. This concept is aligned with Rapha's vision. Rapha Cycle Clubs are

locations where cycling enthusiasts meet to share their love of the sport. The concept Cycle Clubs comes to life with the deployment of concept carriers. In this case, those are campaigns, advertisements, presenters, and of course the content of the programme. Where would you place the Cycle Clubs as concept on the ladder? In this example the concept is highly tangible. That means that under this concept you would not be likely to start developing another café. Therefore, you have few concept carriers and Cycle Club is located low on the ladder. This in contrast to the brand concept of Rapha, under which you could place multiple concept carriers: various programmes, radio, events, online platforms, and promotional activities. Rapha travel is a concept that fits inside the organisational concept of Rapha. With Rapha travel you are also on the road and sharing

>>I ALWAYS SAY: THE ULTIMATE RAPHA PRODUCT IS A HOTEL. IT IS THEN A PLACE TO COME TOGETHER, A PLACE TO SHARE YOUR PASSION. A LUXURY HOTEL, OF COURSE, AS WE ARE A QUALITY BRAND. WE WOULD SERVE CAREFULLY PLANNED DISHES OF HIGH QUALITY IN TERMS OF TASTE AND NUTRITION. A SKI RESORT FOR CYCLISTS.<< Gerben Gerritsen, Rapha

your cycling passion during your holidays. In each product by Rapha a story can be discovered. Those stories are written by them and contribute to the overarching ideas of the brand concept. It makes the product special and unique, and as such contributes to the quality perception. Rapha also has its own magazine. Here again the sharing of passion for the sport is the focal point: for them it is first and foremost about the content – the story – and only after that about the design.

Layers in concepts are challenging material. Each example is different and you cannot place the subject in a fixed framework. Therefore, we would like to offer another example, the concept of the Dutch theme park Efteling: World of Wonders. This is an emotional concept, as it is not tangible. This concept can be shaped in many different ways and is therefore located high on the ladder. Efteling believes that people should be able to escape reality from time to time. On the basis of this idea, you can develop various other concepts,

for instance by offering people entertainment in a fairytale-like manner. The core values of Efteling are quality, uniqueness, and creativity. Raveleijn is a concept that falls under the main concept of Efteling. Raveleijn is a magical town in Efteling. Here a park show is run five times per day, but this town has more to offer than that. It also houses hotel and catering venues and there is an event location. Raveleijn is aligned with Efteling's values and offers people entertainment in a fairytale-like manner. Due to the shape of the concept carriers – a park show, a site, hotel and catering venues, and a TV series – the concept of Raveleijn has come to life.

2.8.1 TYPE OF CONCEPTS IN THE CREATIVE INDUSTRY

In practice, we notice that we mainly deal with concepts for which a higher concept already exists. This situation simply occurs more often because the dormant concept at the highest level of abstraction, including the vision and the core values of the organisation, is fixed for a longer term. For every new concept lower down the ladder a new dormant concept will have to be developed that will eventually have to be in line with the highest located concept (the brand concept or organisational concept). Within the scope of your previously made strategic choices you can develop a new vision on a component inside it, of course again with inclusion of symbolic value. In addition, this book approaches concept thinking from either the strengthening of an already existing concept at a higher or lower level or the creation of a new concept. Creating a new concept will, as mentioned, in most cases concern concepts lower down the ladder.

A social concept is a type of concept that contributes to sustainable solutions for social challenges such as climate change, security, mobility, and renewable energy. For these concepts the principle of concept thinking also applies, seeing as these concepts explicitly generate meaning and do not have the creation of economic value as their primary goal.

Back to the classification of the creative industry. Within the policy of the creative industry we largely see crossover concepts. These are concepts that are generally more similar to product innovation, although they mostly are a logical result from a vision. These crossovers would therefore be fine examples of the living concept in our theory, as they match the dormant concept. This dormant concept, the vision, is then mainly based on creating social value and creates meaning in that manner. If you go back to our definition of the creative industry, we focus on meaningful concepts based on creating symbolic value. After all, we stated

earlier that a concept generates meaning and that this must be communicated. That does not mean that the same concept is not characterised by functional properties, but the starting point of concept thinking is that it creates meaning. This is achieved by the development, framing, and activation of creative, meaningful content and design. Depending on the domain in which the concept is developed, the living concept – the concept carriers – will be shaped differently. This is contextual in nature and the choices therefore lie in the analysis of the dormant concept. Thus we can distinguish many types of concepts. It does not matter so much for the principle of concept thinking what the type of concept is that you wish to work with, as long as the requirement of creating symbolic value is met.

2.9 PRINCIPLES FOR A STRONG CONCEPT

You now know what a concept is. It is also good to know what a strong concept looks like. A strong concept creates and communicates meaning, which ensures a meaningful experience for the consumer. The most important focal points:

ALIGNS WITH THE VISION & SYMBOLIC CORE VALUES. Both in the dormant concept and in the living concept, the vision needs to be reflected clearly. On the basis of the vision, the concept must consistently be implemented in all concept carriers, existing and/or new products and services. The communication must be integrated and consistent at all levels and in all instruments, so that synergy is created. For instance, the vision is continually emphasised and communicated. In this manner, the symbolic values of the consumer are also responded to and the concept is given meaning.

GENERATES ATTENTION. A strong concept sticks in your mind, as you need to attract the consumer's attention. After all, in our current society we have an 'overload' of words and images. We live in an age of abundance, so you need to look for attention. The creative industry is also an attention economy: you need to stand out. Among other ways, you can achieve this by means of the scarcity principle. This creates attention and sparks conversations. Scarcity makes something happen in people's brains, which makes them want the product or service even more. In order to escape the abundance in the attention economy, you need to ensure that people are talking about you. For instance, lifestyle magazine Blend introduced an original concept some years ago: it made good use of scarcity of time and place by opening a number of guerrilla stores. These shops offered interesting brands for a maximum of sixty days and were then immediately closed again. Thus, adding a time limit to promotions is also a good way to generate attention. If consumers then start talking about your product – both online and offline – you are right where you want to be. A concept has to affect something in them, move them emotionally. The consumer needs to want to spend time on it, completely getting immersed by the experience. But even that in itself is not enough: he or she also needs to be prepared to share his or her experience with others, so that the attention is shared.

SPARKS CONVERSATION. A strong concept should not only move and remain interesting, but it also needs to spark conversation. It has a social character. The consumers then ensure that the concept further develops and gets much bigger. Perhaps it invites the consumer to get involved in the thinking process, so that he or she becomes part of the concept. Not until users are talking about it, does it constitute a good concept. By means of constant interaction, the concept is given increasing meaning. Interaction is always happening: between two people, between a person and a group of people, or between a person and a physical product. Thus the concept organises conversations.

FITS THE ORGANISATION. Every organisation has its own personality, its own character, and its own history. The concept needs to fit in with that, as that will ensure authenticity. If an organisation develops a concept that is not directly meant for a certain target group, then

>>IT IS ABOUT ATTENTION, PEOPLE NOTICING YOUR THING. BUT NOT JUST NOTICING; THEY ALSO NEED TO BE PREPARED TO SHARE IT WITH OTHERS, SO THAT THE ATTENTION IS SHARED.<< Arjo Klamer, Erasmus University Rotterdam.

>>A CONCEPT WITHOUT CONVERSATION
IS NOTHING. YOU AND I CAN THINK OF
A CONCEPT, BUT IT IS CRUCIAL THAT
IT IS TALKED ABOUT BY OTHERS.<<

Arjo Klamer, Erasmus University Rotterdam

its own identity is the point of departure. The organisation will then automatically get an audience: people who want to be associated with the vision. These people identify with the vision and the concept.

IS EASY TO UNDERSTAND AND EXPLAIN. Users need to be able to easily find the essence of the concept and as a provider you also need to be able to explain the concept in one sentence. Imagine that you need to store your concept in a moving container with many other concepts and you are not permitted to add the name of your company. What would then be that one sentence that you would write on the box?

GOES TOGETHER WITH THE POWER OF LANGUAGE (IN WORDS AND IMAGES). Language is an important part of a strong concept and ensures that we can convey the concept. Language is communication and emotion. You convey your thoughts to others by means of language. And a good message is convincing, sticks, and fascinates. A clever choice of words that covers the essence of the concept is highly important in this. Language and perception are connected and you can play with this as a concept thinker. People interpret language in various manners, which is why language has depth. People visualise language in personal images and in that manner draw meaning from words. If language and visuals are combined effectively, they reinforce each other. Together they make up an appealing whole, which makes you think and triggers your imagination. In translating the concept into the awakening concept, you therefore need to carefully consider your word and image choices. You dormant concept helps you in doing so. What is your vision? What target group do you wish to address? This will determine what words you use in your awakening concept. Will you opt for the English language, which often occurs in concepts, or will you choose a local language, for instance Dutch in the Netherlands? Does your word choice cover that which you wish to communicate? Sometimes a poor title still perfectly covers the essence of what you wish to convey. For example, this was the case for the TV programme *De slechtste chauffeur van Nederland* [The worst driver of the Netherlands]. That was exactly what it was, no more and no less. In addition, it fits with the way in which BNN (a public broadcaster for youth in the Netherlands) communicates: clearly, briefly, and concisely.

IS RECOGNISABLE. A good concept ensures that whenever the user sees, experiences, or feels something, he or she immediately knows that it belongs to the brand in question or the organisation behind it. The concept ensures that all recognisable loose elements come together under one umbrella.

HAS A LONG SHELF LIFE. An idea is like a mayfly: beautiful, but with a regrettably short lifespan. A concept is like a chameleon: perseverant and able to survive in complete harmony with its environment. An effective concept therefore is aligned with earlier campaigns, products and/or services and offers ample space for continued development. The concept is in line with the circular economy: not just because its raw materials can be reused, but also because it has endurance and thus has the capacity to adjust to new insights and developments. A concept always offers space and is always a piece of a puzzle which can be moved around and used for further expanding the concept. A strong concept is not static, but offers space for further development. It is important not to get stuck in a rigid mould, as this is limiting. The world is not static and therefore concepts should not be either. A concept should not already be outdated by the time it is introduced; it must respond to the advancing time and the advancing insights.

IS FREE OF DISCIPLINE. The world is increasingly hybrid and specialisations are increasingly fused. Concepts must be able to handle the complexity of today, but also that of tomorrow. Geoff Maree, lecturer Imagineering at NHTV Breda University of Applied Sciences, was asked to design the cemetery of 'tomorrow'. The cemetery was allowed to be different from the traditional headstones and urns the supplier had been using up to then. The ultimate solution was much broader: tombstones with small TVs in them. These monitors were linked to an Internet page on which children could for instance upload new drawings for grandpa and grandma, which could then again be placed on the cemetery. This is an example of a cross-border concept that constitutes an improvement of the old granite stone. You start analysing the intention of the cemetery, and that intention is to stimulate and enhance engagement between people and with the deceased.

The secret of a strong concept is hidden in all these principles, but it remains to be seen whether you need to meet all of these criteria in order to arrive at a strong concept. We believe it is most important for your concept to be aligned with your vision and symbolic core values at any given time. The more of the above principles additionally reflected in your concept, the stronger it will become. Upon testing your concept, take these focal points into consideration. We will get back to this in chapters 5 and 6.

CONCEPT THINKING

CONCEPT THINKING

On the one hand, concept thinking takes the needs of the consumers and users as a starting point. On the other hand, new combinations are sought to arrive at products and services that have not yet been recognised as a need by the consumer. The road towards a perfect concept is long. The kitchen assistant will not be able to produce a masterpiece dish on his or her very first working day. However, the chef selects his or her ingredients on the basis of years of experience. Everything is balanced out, so that the guests experience a true taste sensation. Thus, you need to be able to taste the culinary philosophy of the chef in the dish. The waiters will also contribute by serving the meal in line with this philosophy. Only then will the chef be able to welcome his or her guests back. The producers of our time are faced with a similar challenge. This entire process is also referred to as concept development. Whenever we use the terms concept development and concept thinking in this book, both instances are about the manner in which a concept emerges. In other words, concept thinking is our method to achieve concept development. Thus, we developed the idea of a concept as a noun into an activity, an action, and a way of thinking or looking: concept thinking. Concept thinking not only consists of thinking, but also of action. After all, concepts are not just creative in nature. They will also have to be implemented and activated, and this means that effective entrepreneurship is an important skill that should not be overlooked in the principle of concept thinking. In addition to a creative mindset, you also need a social and business mindset. In this chapter we will zoom in on the principle of concept thinking. That means that we will be looking at context, the place where concept thinking starts. In addition, we highlight the terms 'content' and 'design'. Content and design shape the substance and symbolism of the concept. Thus they are important elements for creating a meaningful concept. Design is applied to convey the implicit and explicit message or meaning. The products and services of the concept are purchased by consumers because they evoke meaning for people. On the basis of that an experience emerges. In order to better understand the term 'experience', we briefly discuss the terms perception and experience.

3.1 THE FIELD OF CONCEPT THINKING

Concept thinking is a relatively new field and little has been written on it so far. Indeed, there is limited literature on concept development. Considering the developments in society and the incredible growth of the field, the subject actually requires further and in-depth explanation compared to the previously published book. Concept development is not a traditional field such as marketing or branding, on which a huge body of literature can be found. Marketing, branding, and concept development are all located within the same paradigm, but offer different perspectives within this paradigm. We create nuances in order to enhance the multidimensional character of these fields of expertise. The challenges from the actual practice are often too complex to handle with a one-dimensional approach. It is not our ambition to position the disciplines in respect to each other. We do want to focus on the similarities, which will make the essence of the separate disciplines comprehensible quicker and more thoroughly. With concept thinking we have already formed a vision regarding the adjacent fields of expertise that overlap. We see concept thinking as a component of branding. You could also refer to it as a concept brand. Whenever the concept of a brand is referred to, it is often about that which we define as the dormant concept. When marketing is discussed, it refers to marketing of the living concept. A concept brand is a brand that distinguishes itself in terms of psychosocial meaning. That means that the consumer can demonstrate who he or she is by means of the use of the living concept. We consider this an important component of concept thinking. Before we further explain the principle of concept thinking, we first focus on the terms 'perception' and 'experience'. After all, with a concept we strive to affect symbolic value creation, and within the creative industry this is mostly done by creating a meaningful experience. But what is that exactly?

3.2 PERCEPTION AND EXPERIENCE

A brief definition of perception according to Macmillan Dictionary is 'a particular way of understanding or thinking about something,' which is in essence an inner experience. The terms 'perception' and 'experience' determine the perspective from which the experience is considered. It clarifies whether it is about the consumer or the demand. If it is about the consumer, we use the term 'perception'. The customer has a perception of something, and thus perceives it in a certain way. Concepts do not arrive at their full meaning or value, until they interact with an individual, as demonstrated in chapter 2. Value, and therefore perception, is relative and is determined contextually. It is the subjetive, inner response to a certain stimulus. The psychosocial framework of the individual determines how the extrinsic value, and thus eventually symbolic individual value, is processed. As a result, the optimal processing of content is different for every individual and is determined by a number of factors. Emotion and cognition

are of influence here, as well as the social context of the individual. In chapter 6 we will further discuss the processing of the concept by the consumer.

The term 'experience' is used when we refer to the stimulus itself. In this case, it also refers to the producer (the offer): the company offers an experience. The confrontation of the consumer with this experience generates a perception. This therefore creates a subdivision in the term 'experience': experience as the stimulus and experience as the internal response to this. We will now go deeper into a meaningful experience as stimulus, because this book is focused on people occupied with creating concepts.

When is a concept meaningful? It is meaningful when it does not only satisfy its functional value, but also the symbolic one. This value is that bit more intensive: the consumer identifies with the concept. In chapter 2 you were able to read that the term 'symbolic value' is not easily captured in a description. We have fine-tuned it further and in doing so made a meaningful experience dependent on the individual symbolic value attributed by the individual to the separate components of the notion. A meaningful concept confirms what is already your view: it is important to you and you recognise that in something you go through. Literally, giving meaning means: contextualising information in a network of existing knowledge. Can I make sense of it? Whether a consumer can do so depends on the individual value. However, it can also occur that the stimulus is processed in such a way that it leads to awareness or meaning. It differs for each individual when something is meaningful or not. Anna Snel (interview 2014) describes this as follows: the individual who experiences the concept determines the meaning, not the producer. According to Snel, the most important thing a producer can do is pay attention to people. People want to experience the story of the concept in every interaction with the concept. We call this experience design. As a producer of an experience you certainly influence this, but creating an effective experience is only possible if you listen attentively to the consumer. In order to activate the selected dimension of the symbolic value as powerfully as possible, you need to thoroughly observe at what stage of the concept this originates. For instance, the basis for the identity value as a dimension will reside in the dormant concept. As a producer, you create your creative content on the basis of this deconstruction of symbolic value. You eventually translate this content into a design for the living concept that contributes to the symbolic value, which you will have determined in advance. This ensures that it becomes a meaningful experience. We use the terminology from Anna Snel (2014) here, in which an experience can be meaningful or integrative. For this book we will not discuss integrative experiences. We assume that in creating a concept you create a meaningful experience, in which the intrinsic value of the consumer is actively relied on. In some cases there will only be an emotional experience. This is an independent perception that at the moment of experience provides a nice, pleasant, beautiful, or sad feeling, but generates no further meaning beyond that.

3.3 WHAT IS CONCEPT THINKING?

Concept thinking is a train ride that never really ends. That train ride does not occur linearly, as is usual, but crisscross throughout the entire country. The stations might well be familiar, but that does not apply to the route and the 'logical' order. What do we mean by this? Concept thinking is an iterative process, a process that never stops. You hop on board somewhere and start the journey, on your way to the next station. If you forget your bag somewhere, you need to get back to the start, as you cannot get anywhere without your baggage. In other words: you go through various phases in order to arrive at a concept and this is not always a linear process. You start or end up somewhere, but often you need to retrace all your steps or zoom in on a certain step before you can continue on. For instance, you need to reflect on your ideas in light of your vision along the way before you can resume your journey. In concept thinking you are continually zooming in and out - testing. On the road to your vision, the dormant concept, you always take some time to zoom in on your previous step, for instance on the environment analysis or the consumer analysis you made. Is your dormant concept still aligned with the analysis? This also applies for your living concept. After all, you do not develop your living concept independently from your dormant and awakening concept. On the contrary, they need each other. If anything changes anywhere, this has consequences for the other stages within the concept.

The core of concept thinking is that the term 'value' is given a broader meaning: the perspective of meaning is considered in a strategic manner. This can have either an internal or an external focus, or a combination of both. Concept thinking is a way of thinking to create symbolic value in a manner that allows consumers to undergo a meaningful experience. It is concerned with the skill to identify patterns and opportunities – thus analytic thinking. In order to do so you use your left brain hemisphere. With the qualities of your right brain

> **>>GOOD HUMAN RELATIONSHIPS ARE THE KEY TO SUCCESS.<<** Fredrik Öst, SNASK

– inventiveness, empathy, and attributing meaning – you build a story around this. By combining your two brain hemispheres a new possibility emerges, partly due to the influence of your right brain hemisphere. In this context problems are no longer problems, but opportunities and possibilities. Creativity is therefore, as demonstrated earlier, important in concept thinking. It is a holistic way of looking. You see connections between things and observe the whole. Everything is interconnected and loose elements are part of something bigger. Within concept thinking you develop a vision and at the highest level of abstraction this vision is not tied to a discipline.

We are now focusing on content and design, substance followed by function and form by means of content and design. We are aware of the fact that we could also direct our focus differently. For instance, in America we often saw another approach, in which form was followed by content. The question you could ask yourself as a concept developer is: are you working from a feeling or are you working towards a feeling? If you work on the basis of a feeling, you work highly intuitively and will sooner be inclined to start with form. However, in most cases we see that concept developers often start with content, from analysis, and later translate this into a form. In concept thinking we are not only innovating, but also telling stories and creating meaningful expe-

riences. We want to tell a story by means of the concept to all stakeholders that come in touch with the concept. These stories can be told at various moments and places. This is also referred to as (story) layers in concepts. The term concept thinking inherently also contains the term 'concept action', which is to say that you do not make your vision tangible unless you implement and activate something in the living concept. Moreover, in concept thinking we do not consider the consumer exclusively as a buyer, but as someone with whom we wish to build, maintain, and deepen a relationship. The crux of the matter therefore lies in paying attention to people. Concept thinking can take place both inside-out and outside-in. You take the identity of the organisation as your starting point but are also aware of the wishes and needs of the stakeholders and what goes on in society. These two points of principles are constantly moving. As a concept developer you jump back and forth between these two approaches.

3.3.1 HOW TO GET FROM DORMANT TO LIVING?

Section 3.3 demonstrated that concept thinking is iterative and therefore dynamic. The stages overlap and you continually need to assess whether the overall picture still makes sense. After all, it is all about getting that overall picture to fit just right! Getting the pieces to fit just right in the overall picture is what generates

CONCEPT THINKING = THE DEVELOPMENT+ THE FRAMING + THE ACTIVATION OF THE SYMBOLIC VALUE BY MEANS OF CREATIVE MEANINGFUL CONTENT AND DESIGN.

meaning. Concept thinking is a way of thinking in which you continually try to complete the puzzle. You look for the constant fit of all three stages. If somewhere in one of the stages something changes, this has consequences for the other stages. In addition, you carry the previous stages with you in making new choices. In chapter 2 you could read that a concept consists of three stages: dormant, awakening, and living. The stages of a concept are interlinked; they need each other. They meet in the middle and that is where meaning emerges. A living concept has no body without an awakening and dormant part. Even before you start with the development of the first stage, the dormant

concept, you need to know what your starting point is. You need to understand where on the ladder the concept is located and what the impetus is that sets the process in motion.

Figure 3.1 demonstrates that the stages of the dormant, awakening, and living concept are interconnected. The connecting factors are content and design: together they create meaning. In the following sections these terms will be further explained. Despite the dynamic character of concept thinking, it always starts with something you see and experience in context. You are triggered by a question, opportunity, possibility, change, development, or problem. With context we here refer to the organisation, the consumer, or the environment. This trigger moment results in an imbalance in one of the stages of the concept. With this 'trigger' the process of concept thinking starts.

You see something in the context, are triggered by a question/opportunity/possibility/problem or situation within the organisation, for the consumer, in the environment, or in a combination of these. You determine where in the three stages of concept thinking this 'trigger' emerges and where on the concept ladder this situation is presenting itself. In order to answer this

effectively, you check whether there is already a higher concept. If an organisation already has a concept, this means that you will be developing a new concept with an accompanying vision within the already existing vision and higher concept. If there is no higher concept yet, you need to create everything from start to finish. To this end, you will be zooming in and out. This generally means that you will quickly end up at the dormant concept. By means of a number of examples, we will demonstrate this principle of zooming in and out.

Figure 3.1 Dynamic Concept Code Model

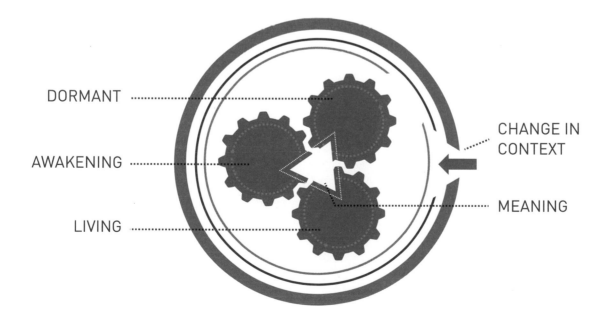

DORMANT

AWAKENING

LIVING

CHANGE IN CONTEXT

MEANING

• 5 years ago, Marten Blankesteijn was standing in front of a magazine holder in the supermarket, not knowing which magazine to choose. Every magazine contained something that interested him. This was the trigger for Marten to further consider this challenge. He saw something in his environment and ascertained as a consumer that not one of the magazines offered everything he wanted. In this case, there was no concept to speak of yet, neither higher nor lower on the ladder. With this trigger as his starting point, Marten developed a new concept: Blendle. After further analysis and research the dormant concept emerged in all likelihood: selling paid journalism in another way. The concept is ideal for those who do not have a need for a fixed subscription with accompanying waste paper pile, but does appreciate well-written pieces and is prepared to pay for those. In addition, the payment has an added friendly feature: if you do not like the piece, you get your money back. This thus shapes the business model and the name Blendle completes the awakening concept. The living concept is primarily the application developed for Blendle, but this idea would also enable you to shape multiple concept carriers.

• In 2013, nine years after 'Sense and Simplicity', Philips introduced a new slogan. The awakening concept of Philips changed with it. Philips wished to be up to date with regard to the needs of consumers and embrace changes in its environment. Philips saw that innovation needed to contribute more to the improvement of the lives of people and that it was no longer just about launching new products from a technological inventions standpoint. It was time for a new positioning. This was captured in 2013 in: 'Philips, innovation and you'. This rebranding also meant a new logo design. The new logo design had to be appropriate for digital use, but also still draw on its well-known shield and thus fit into the vision and the brand concept of Philips. Philips believes that there is always a way to improve life. The adjustment they made in the awakening concept thus also needed to be aligned with Philips' dormant concept in this case. Ultimately, all three stages needed to be realigned.

• In some situations you will see something in context that you can immediately implement in the living concept. This is the case in the above-mentioned example from section 1.3.3: Disney's MagicBand. The development of the continually connected smartphone is more driven by technology in our lives. There is a continually increasing number of applications that we wear close to the skin: wearables are the most intimate 'touchpoints' that are increasingly unlocking the digital world. Personal behaviour determines the information that is displayed. Maintaining a constant data dialogue responds to the needs of the consumer to add something in the customer journey at the moment it adds value to the consumer. This development also did not go unnoticed by Disney. The introduction of the Magic-Bands responds to this. You can use the bracelets for everything in the park; it is a new payment method on that basis of profiles and actual use. You could also add new features, such as stimulating healthy behaviour. For example, those with a high step count could be given a discount in the restaurant. However, you only offer access to services that are relevant to your customers' needs at that moment. In this situation the trigger emerged in the living concept of Disney. The application of the MagicBand therefore has to be aligned with the dormant concept of Disney. Security is one of the most important, perhaps the top, core values of Disney. The Magic Band is excellently aligned with this, as a visitor you no longer have to carry around money or cards due to the introduction of this payment method. This gives visitors a feeling of safety and freedom, which allows them to enjoy all that Disney has to offer even more.

The three examples demonstrate that the kind of trigger from the context determines which stage of the concept gets imbalanced. At the same time, you can also see that you will always circle back to the dormant concept. That is hardly surprising, especially if you consider that the trigger results from the context and that that same context forms the basis on which the dormant concept was developed. In sum: it is primarily important to identify in what stage you are and where on the ladder the stage is located, so that you do not lose sight of the coherence of your concept. Depending on the location, you assess on the basis of the dormant concept. This is highly important in the concept development process. Is your dormant concept still aligned with the analysis, your trigger? If your answer is negative, then have another look at the dormant concept. If the answer is affirmative, then you can again zoom out and take the next step: the awakening concept. You now have a starting point for further design. Zooming in and out is thus a constant practice, at every stage. If you make the concept living, you will also again have to take a critical look at whether it fits with your dormant concept. Zooming in and out is crucial and therefore makes the

>>WE WERE FOUNDED ON THE BASIS OF A FRUSTRATION OF SORTS. DURING THE WEEK, YOU PAY CAREFUL ATTENTION TO YOUR CLOTHING, BUT AS SOON AS YOU GET ON THAT BICYCLE, YOU WOULD WEAR A HORRENDOUS CYCLING SHIRT WITH A LOGO OF THE LOCAL PLUMBING COMPANY OR BUTCHER ON IT. WE THEN STARTING THINKING FROM THE IDEA: "I WANT TO CYCLE IN QUALITY GEAR". THUS WE STARTED FROM A PLACE OF PASSION.<<

Gerben Gerritsen, Rapha

process iterative. The dormant concept can be seen as conditional for the other two stages.

3.4 CONTEXT

As already described above, a trigger in the context always provides the impetus for concept thinking. Therefore, we will take a moment to zoom in on the definition of the term of 'context' and demonstrate from what perspectives we look at this term in this book. We consider context to be the total environment in which something receives meaning, or in other words: the background or frame of reference. It is about holistic coherence between the changing world, consumers, and the organisation. As an organisation you enter into a one-on-one relationship with the consumer and therefore you need to have knowledge of both your own organisation and the continually changing environment in which the organisation and the consumer are located. The change/opportunity or impetus that you see in the context thus comes from either the changing outside world, the organisation itself, or the consumer. You could consider these elements (organisation, environment analysis, and consumer) within the context as various powers that influence the overall concept. As mentioned earlier, if anything changes in one of the three powers, a new fit needs to be sought. The three powers have a continual influence on each other. It is about the adaptability of the organisation, in addition to which the environment and the consumer need to be paid attention to.

The environmental analysis and the consumer can be seen as the external side of the context; the organisation itself is an internal aspect. On the external side, the influences come from the outside. As an organisation you cannot always directly influence this. The internal aspect of the context, the organisation itself, can be influenced, as it concerns the internal organisation. Below, you will find a brief description per element. In the chapter on the dormant concept we will concretely deal with how you can shape these elements.

ORGANISATIONAL ANALYSIS

Who and what is the organisation exactly? What mission, vision, and core values does the organisation have? And how is this implemented both internally and externally? In this element you search for the identity of the organisation. That identity can be made clear in multiple ways. For instance, the history, culture, core values, vision, and the manner in which the organisation positions itself are important. For a not yet existing concept, the identity of the beginning entrepreneur needs to be shaped. If there is an already existing concept, it is important to align with the identity of an existing organisation with already existing concept carriers. For a beginning organisation there is not yet any prior history and culture, which means the focus is thus rather on the personal values of the entrepreneur. It is important to find out what makes this organisation different from other organisations. In order to appear authentic, it is important that the identity and image of the organisation correspond to the extent possible. Successes and failures determine the impression you make on your stakeholders. As an organisation you need to deliver on your promises and meet the expectations of your stakeholders. As a concept thinker it is important to know these types of things, because you lose credibility if your concept does not match your organisation.

If something changes within their organisation and a question or opportunity arises, concept thinkers take this as their starting point. An example of a change/opportunity from inside the organisation can be for instance that the identity does not correspond to an image that the organisation/concept brand has.

CONSUMER ANALYSIS

What concerns consumers? What do they like and what do they worry about? As an organisation you will want to attract the attention of consumers and ensure that they connect with your concept. You wish to understand the mindset of your consumers in order to create something that suits them. It is important to pay individual attention to the consumer. It is increasingly hard to find out what the consumer thinks or feels. Consumers will also have different needs and emotions in different situations. Often, consumers are not able to indicate their own needs, which means you cannot solely respond to what they are saying: you also need some sensitivity. You need to be able to sense the market and search for subjective experiences and perceptions of the consumer. The purchasing behaviour of consumers is determined by the values he or she strives for.

If you start researching the consumer behaviour, you will quickly find out that the individuals of today can no longer be considered uniform. You can no longer say: I am a married man and have two children. No, nowadays you are a cooking enthusiast, painter, architect, runner and father of Finn and Sep. You consider freedom and happiness important and identify with passions and values that best describe you. The one moment you are eating at a bistro, because you are on a fun family outing for a day; the next moment you are on the road with your client and dining in style in a restaurant with a Michelin star. As a consumer you thus function within various situations and belong to various groups. In every group you also have a different role. Due to these dynamics it is difficult to place a consumer in one target group and discover a pattern in consumer behaviour. We should no longer approach the consumer exclusively as a buyer, but as someone with whom we wish to build, maintain, and deepen a relationship. It is about the demand and the need underlying that demand: the use value and symbolic value. In order to find this out, you do not just look at the consumer 'outsights', but also at insights. This means that you also need to consider that which the consumer cannot or does not want to tell, which emerges from looking at the behaviour of the consumer. Thus, you need insight into situation and behaviour.

As soon as you notice that there is a change in need among consumers, the concept becomes imbalanced and action will be required from you. This need can be signalled from inside the organisation or ascertained by a concept thinker. It is important to take the need of the consumer as your point of departure instead of the demand. The demand is often a product/service, but it is important to ask yourself what the need is that underlies this. The context of the consumers – where they live, with what values they were raised, thus the culture of their country – determines how consumers consume. In developing a concept, it is important to be conscious of what your target group is, and that it is likely to be an international audience. Under the influence of globalisation borders are blurring, which means consumers increasingly encounter foreign/other cultures. These cultures increasingly form a source of inspiration, which can change the needs of the consumer. After all, as consumers we feel attracted to various aspects of other cultures. We should take this into account in the development of our concepts.

ENVIRONMENT ANALYSIS

The world is changing increasingly fast and ensures that our living environment constantly changes in appearance. We know that everything changes and nothing is truly permanent. These changes also cause our attitude regarding society to change. This changing attitude, in turn, has its consequences for the choices we make. Do we find a concept appealing or not? Do we wish to abolish certain products? Viewing trends is an important part of the environment analysis. A clear vision is based on what goes on in society, which requires you to keep an eye on what happens. You can picture a trend as a mentality or behavioural change, a wave-like movement, or a rising and falling development line. The values of consumers change continually and you can respond to this with your concept by adding meaning to it. Trends are considered opportunities to respond to. Trend research provides up-to-date insight into the market in which you operate. There are various ways to look at trends: at a market level (micro trends), at a consumer level, and at a societal level. The trends at a consumer level are those on the basis of which you develop a concept, among other things; they are the medium-term trends. For consumer trends it is about the wishes, needs, and desires of the consumer, and therefore it will most likely fall under consumer analysis. It is hereby no longer about just the product, but also about the wishes, needs, and desires of the consumer. These trends are focused on the changes in perception. In addition to these trends, there are

also constantly developments that may or may not influence your concept, and thus to which you can or can not respond. For instance, there are developments which you as a concept developer cannot influence, but there are also developments that will trigger you to review your concept. For example, technological, social and ecological developments. Competitors also fall inside the scope of environment analysis. Thus, keep looking around you, keep an eye on what the market does, and keep standing out as an organisation. In the environment analysis you will mainly look at micro trends, short-term trends. These trends primarily influence the living concept and cause a change at the product/service level, an adjustment or an addition.

3.5 CONTENT AND DESIGN, OUTPUT OF CONCEPT THINKING

The statement that we wish to substantiate in this book is that design and content play a vital role in the development of a concept. The creative industry is design-driven (Rutten, 2014). All creative subsectors mainly focus on design. For instance, the media and entertainment industry, where it is all about the design of new formats. In the subsector of arts and culture it is mainly about the aesthetic expression of the design. Various forms of design are classified as creative business services. All these design activities are considered part of the creative industry, but the type of design activity determines at what stage of the concept design it can be found. However, not only the external manifestation, but also the idea it contains is important. The story or the creative vision (shape, content, and function) forms an indivisible whole; the three components are like cause and effect. The stages of the dormant, awakening, and living concept are interconnected by means of the output of content and design. Content and design overlap the stages and ensure that the concept becomes a whole. Developing meaning, framing meaning, activating meaning: these are the consecutive actions you go through within the stages of a concept. In their mutual coherence, content and design ensure a meaningful experience, for which we consider design in the context of concept thinking to be form and content to be the substance that is decisive for the form. The function of the concept lies hidden in both content and design. This is one perspective: do you create a feeling or meaning on the basis of content, or do you start out with a feeling and thus rather with design? In various interviews in the US and beyond, it was striking to see that in some cases design was taken as the starting point for developing concepts, from which the content would emerge later. This contradicts the manner in which most concept developers in Europe work. As a concept developer you thus have your own style. Each concept thinker is different and goes through the development process in their unique manner. For instance, you could be highly analytical or rather more intuitive. From these varying perspectives, the model can also be applied in various ways. An element can be left out or rather be given more emphasis. The biggest contrast is provided by comparing the intuitive manner with the analytical manner of concept thinking. By juxtaposing these two extremes, you can assess what appeals most to you. Someone who works more intuitively will place a great emphasis on dreaming, allowing for all possibilities: that allows you to dream away by using your imagination and design then takes centre stage. A more analytical person will apply dreaming in a different manner, for instance in order to

get aligned with the client. It is important that you as a concept thinker apply a style that suits your personality or the company you work for. This book takes the most common method as its point of departure, in which content is followed by form and design results from content. Ellen Schindler from kossmann.dejong says: 'Narration is the sum of translation and design.' We have adjusted this slightly: concept thinking is the sum of narration, translation, and imagination. In order to be able to put this into practice, there are elements you cover per stage. These are further elaborated on per stage in the following chapters. Before we get started with this, we will first dive a little deeper into the terms 'content' and 'design'. Form and content thus make up an indivisible whole, from formulation to imagination, which is focused on evoking a meaningful experience for people.

3.6 WHAT IS CONTENT?

Content is a label that is stuck to everything and anything and regularly causes confusion. If you look at the various definitions that apply to the term 'content', you must conclude that the term is multi-interpretable. Literally, 'content' refers to contents, something that is contained in something else. According to the dictionary, content is any collection of writing, pictures, animations, etc. offered on- and offline. Bob Boiko, the author of *The Content Management Bible*, attributes a different definition to content: 'Content is the information and interactivity that organisations must apply to be deliver value to their customers.' Content concerns all contents and interactivity with which value is delivered through all channels and it serves a goal. This book considers content through the lens of communication.

We now know that you can communicate meaning with concept thinking by means of a meaningful experience. In doing so, it is about conveying the mindset that contributes to the identity and long-term objectives of an organisation, in which the consumer is never left out of consideration. In this book we apply a definition of the term 'content' that is connected to the definition of concept thinking. Seeing as a concept always communicates meaning, the content of a concept is at least communicative in nature. In the above we wrote that the symbolic value cannot be disconnected from the functional value of a concept, as it is a combination of the demand and needs of the consumer. The communicative aspect is based on the extrinsic symbolic value, as described in chapter 2. This is predominantly developed in the dormant concept at a higher level of abstraction. A concept can, as demonstrated earlier, be developed at a lower level, but even then the content will be aligned with the dormant concept at a higher level and therefore always be communicative in nature.

3.6.1 IMPORTANCE OF CONTENT

In our current society, content is a highly effective tool for attracting consumers/stakeholders, receiving loyalty from them, and spark interaction from them. Organisations take content as their point of departure and shape their concept carriers accordingly. Addressing the right people with the right content, at the right moment and for the right reasons is important. Thus, it is all about WHAT you want to say, to WHOM, WHY and HOW you wish to say it. It is about that which you wish to offer the consumer and what they can subsequently experience. This means that the way in which the consumer receives and processes content plays an important role in the creation of content. It is not only about broadcasting, but actually about the interaction or dialogue that your have with the consumer. The effect of the content on the consumer can cause the process of content development to be reshaped from the higher level of the dormant concept. If the content of a concept does not correspond to how the executed concept is experienced by people, it is not viable. Similarly, if such a concept is not aligned with environmental factors in which it is placed, it will fail. The content is thus developed in relation to the context. Content development is therefore a prerequisite for design and thus for the development of your overall concept.

3.6.2 CONTENT PER STAGE

Content consists of a number of components, which can be linked to the stages of a concept. You can ask yourself whether the intended stimulus per phase is also received as a response. The manner in which content is processed determines the manner in which consumers perceive the experience. This can differ per individual and depends on the psychological frame of reference of the individual, as demonstrated in section 3.2. In particular, the individual values (emotional, cognitive values) that are attributed to the individual are decisive in this. In addition, the social context of the individual plays a big role. The consumer cannot engage in interaction with the stimulus, unless he or she actually has a sensory perception of it. This is where content is translated into physical design: in the living concept. Up until the stage of the living concept, content is an internal matter, that which is described in words. Let us revisit the shifts we discussed in chapter and get ahead of design within the dormant concept. Images have a powerful effect as communication medium. For instance, you can use visual language to enforce what you mean, convince or stimulate people, prove or compare things, convey a universal message, and provide insight into complex matters. However, in order to select images, you first need to know what you want to tell. That is why we still often start the process off with written words, the story, and the vision. What vision is important to both the organisation and the target group in creating meaning? These communicative aspects – the story, the vision, and the core values of the dormant concept – jointly determine the content of this stage. In the awakening concept the dormant concept is provided with language, resulting in a name, one-liner, or term. This is where the tone of the content is determined and the first concept directions are come up with and tested. The concretion of the vision is summarised in an action plan. In the awakening concept the type of business model of the concept is also considered. Finally, the living concept determines what you will be communicating where. The living concept determines the physical content, all the so-called touchpoints consumers are confronted with during their customer journey.

3.7 WHAT IS DESIGN?

Design is a word with many definitions. For instance, according the Dutch *Van Dale* dictionary, design is defined as something along the lines of 'an (artistic) industrial design; the style, the shape of a product.' This description links design to the product appearance. We consider this definition too limited, as this would mean that you would only apply design in the living concept. Kapferer (2003) considers design the process of adding value. In order to create such added value, the design must improve the product function for consumers and

CONTENT DORMANT CONCEPT:
COMMUNICATIVE PERCEPTION ASPECTS IN WORDS. THIS INCLUDES SYMBOLIC VALUES, ESSENCE OF THE VISION AND THE (CORPORATE) STORY.

CONTENT AWAKENING CONCEPT:
CONNECTING LANGUAGE TO THE DORMANT CONCEPT BY ADDING SIGNIFIERS: NAMES, WORDS, DEFINITIONS, OBJECTIVES AND TERMS.

CONTENT LIVING CONCEPT:
ALL TOUCHPOINTS PERCEPTIBLE TO THE SENSES THAT THE CONSUMERS ENCOUNTER DURING THEIR CUSTOMER JOURNEY, IN PARTICULAR ON THE BASIS OF FUNCTIONAL ASPECTS.

be meaningful. We live in an environment that is bursting with design. Our environment is entirely designed, whether done well or poorly. Despite the meaning that design adds, it is mostly concerned with functionality. You might wonder what the role of aesthetics/beauty is in this. The idea that added value is also associated with increasing the aesthetic value would certainly be confirmed by designers. Still, this is not commonplace among all concept thinkers. The importance of aesthetic value is certainly not always recognised. The insight that objects can have an emotional impact and therefore an influence on consumer preferences is a component in concepts that should not be underestimated. For instance, the laminated safety instructions of the airline

KLM in their airplane chairs that display what you need to do in case of emergencies. They were made from a functional standpoint, but do they actually serve their purpose? The answer is no. Research has indicated that most passengers never even look at the card, which is why KLM presented a new safety instruction video in November 2015. For this video, as many as a thousand Delftware tiles were painted by hand. It became a video with a typically Dutch appearance. This example illustrates that aesthetics actually support functionality. Design is able to shape the symbolic and functional value of the concept. The term 'design' can refer to the process itself or the result of this process: the physical manifestation. Design is thus not just about external manifestation, but also about the visualisation of the vision. Design enables you to visualise the written word and make it physical. For us, design is the external appearance of content, differentiated per stage.

3.7.1 IMPORTANCE OF DESIGN

We have demonstrated that meaning has become important and that we therefore wish to add meaning to concepts. In addition to story, you can do so by means of design. In that way you make the concept tangible and create aesthetics. Have a good look around you: everything around you is designed and for everything design choices have been made. As a concept developer it is therefore highly important to think in terms of design. You need to visualise your ideas; consider it the materialisation of your concept. Concept developers are not always designers, but knowledge of design does help you a lot in communicating with the parties that will eventually take care of the design for you. You are the director of the activation of the concept. You know the world that you have imagined around the concept as no other, which is why you will be able to make design choices. For instance, think of style, atmosphere, colours, typography, visuals and shapes. You now know that it is important to make these choices on the basis of your vision. Your vision and your concept name are leading in this. Design ensures that the concept becomes perceptible to the senses and therefore determines the success of the concept. In addition to ensuring beauty, and thus fulfilling an aesthetic function, design also contains other functions. In his book *Emotional Design*, Norman (2004) states that the emotional side to design can be even more important for the success of products than the more practical elements. However, we feel that both aspects need to be covered to create an effective concept. Both the demand (mostly

>>TO ME, DESIGN IS NOT JUST THE CREATION OF SOMETHING, BUT ALSO THE CREATION OF CERTAIN COMPANY PROCESSES.<<

Dirk Hens, Butts and Shoulders

the functional value) and the needs (the symbolic value) of the consumer need to be responded to. Norman describes three aspects of design: visceral, behavioural, and reflective design. Visceral design focuses on the appearance, the aesthetic pleasure. At this subconscious level, design can generate desire or temptation. It concerns the direct and emotional impact of appearance, colour, material, and feeling (tactile surface) that is indicated as appeal. The second aspect, behavioural design, focuses on effective use and thus on the degree to which it fulfils utilitarian and functional purposes. Here it is all about function, performance, usability, comprehensibility, and ergonomics. The third aspect, reflective design, is focused on the rationalisation and intellectual satisfaction, or the story that the design conveys. This occurs at the level of consciousness and relates to self-reflection (self-image), personal satisfaction, and memory. Thus, it is about the intellectual and reflective perception of beauty here, the genera-

tion of symbolic value. These three aspects correspond to three layers of the human brain, in which information is processed. The visceral is the lowest level (the simplest, most primitive and sensitive) and the reflective is the highest level, which is only found in humans. According to Norman, you cannot deem a design successful without having incorporated all three design functions. We agree with this. The design functions can be linked to the stages of a concept. Reflective design to the dormant concept, behavioural to the awakening concept, and the visceral to the living concept. Naturally, the first two functions of design can only be observed in the living concept, but they originate in the corresponding stages. The three design components interweave emotion and cognition ('knowing') and thus create emotional and cognitive value, or in other words the individual value as described in chapter 2. According to Norman, emotion is an indivisible and essential part of cognition. Knowledge helps us under-

Figure 3.2 Design Meaning Pyramid

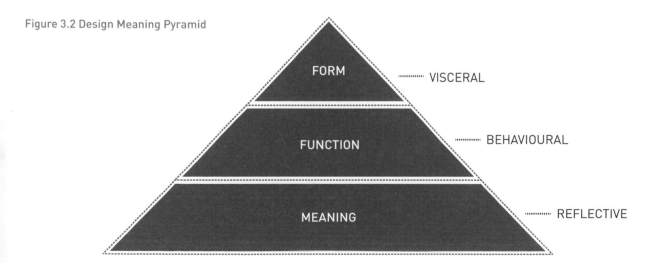

>>DESIGN IS A MINDSET THAT NEEDS TO BE EMBEDDED INTO ORGANIZATIONS TO DELIVER A GREAT CONCEPT.<< Sarah Drummond

stand the world around us, while emotion enables us to make quick decisions. Depending on the strategic choices made in the dormant and awakening concept, you can use design to shape this in your living concept. You can also approach this from another perspective. The three functions of design can be captured in Maslow's pyramid figure 3.2. This pyramid has become too small for our current society. With our desire for meaning we have evolved to an even higher level and transcend Maslow's pyramid. We are personally holding the reigns in creating our own identity and as a concept thinker you need to be conscious of that. If you consider the design perspective from the standpoint of concept thinking, Maslow's pyramid is exactly reversed. Maslow maintains that an individual strives to satisfy the needs according to a fixed a hierarchical pattern. In other words: people experience their higher needs after they have mainly satisfied their lower needs. The first basic level would then be meaning, the idea behind the design. Once meaning has been covered you can continue on, and this is developed in the dormant concept. Moreover, the functional/utilitarian aspect comes in addition to that, i.e. what is the function of the design? This is comparable to behavioural design as described above. Thirdly, we consider aesthetics. Do we find something visually appealing? Here we must emphasis that in some situations products are only purchased on the basis of aesthetics and the intrinsic

value of an object, but a good concept involves fulfilling all three design functions. Later on in chapter 6, we will further deepen our understanding of the three functions by naming all the layers that design entails.

3.7.2 DESIGN PER STAGE

It is increasingly easier to use images in addition to text in order to convey your story. This emerging trend is called visual storytelling. The use of visuals in communication will only increase due to the development of for instance augmented reality and diminished reality, FaceTime, Qwiki and much more. Communication is becoming increasingly visual. This ensures that the more traditional forms of communication are becoming less dominant. Visuals add meaning to the world in which we live, and we give meaning to the visuals. Visual language is not just the catalyst for this process, but at the same time a powerful form of expression for sharing meanings. Design thus plays a highly important role in the dormant concept. If you solely use content you might be faced with some surprises in the living concept, as it often turns out in retrospect that not all parties were speaking the same language in the translation of the content into design. For instance, you can use visual language to enforce what you mean, convince or stimulate people, prove or compare things, convey a universal message, and provide insight into complex matters. You can do so by already visualising your story at the level of the dormant concept; the research you conduct for the content is simultaneously done for design. In the awakening concept these images and atmospheres are converted into a design map that at least displays the typography, colour, and material of the organisational concept or the underlying concept. The living concept it concerned with the creative visualisation of the dormant and the awakening concept. The concept becomes perceptible to the senses by means of a physical and virtual manifestation.

3.8 CHOICE OF CONTENT AND DESIGN

At each stage the choice, the development, the framing, and activation of content and design is based on a number of factors. For instance, you need to know who you are creating the concept for and in what context this concept will appear. Always tailor your content and the design to the target group, but also to the organisation and the domain in which you are creating the concept. Ask yourself what symbolic value you want to create for the consumer and what this is actually based on.

DESIGN DORMANT CONCEPT:
REFLECTIVE DESIGN, THE STORY, YOUR VISION, AND CORE VALUES VISUALISED FLUIDLY.

DESIGN AWAKENING CONCEPT:
BEHAVIOURAL DESIGN, YOUR DESIGN MAP.

DESIGN LIVING CONCEPT:
VISCERAL DESIGN, DESIGN AS PHYSICAL AND VIRTUAL MANIFESTATION.

>>THE CHOICE OF DESIGN IS ALSO RELATED TO THE PRECONDITIONS ALREADY IN PLACE. FOR INSTANCE, YOU WILL NOT COVER THE WALL OF A MUSEUM WITH GOLD, AS THERE SIMPLY IS INSUFFICIENT BUDGET TO DO SO.<<

Mark de Jong, Kosmann.dejong

In other words: how important is the content for the guest? Do you stand out sufficiently and can you also implement and deliver this content as a company, and do you have the right resources to do so? Remember chapter 1, in which we described that there are various organisational connections to be recognised between various activities. The way in which the content is developed and activated can entirely occur in-house, but it can also be the case that as an organisation you only possess the expertise to carry out one of these activities well. Therefore, you need to carefully consider organisational, financial, and technical aspects of design and content before you make a choice. The basis of all choices lies in the development of the dormant concept. What vision and what story is important and suitable for the target groups and the organisation? What meaning do you want to ultimately create as an organisation in order to arrive at a meaningful concept? In other words: what story do you wish to tell? And what does this eventually mean for the awakening and later on the living concept in order to further shape the dormant concept? When you speak of the creation of a concept at a lower level of abstraction, the content will naturally have to be aligned with a higher level of organisational concept.

Content at a lower level than the organisational concept that is not enforced leads to a fragmentation of your concept. In chapters 4 to 6 we will further elaborate on the choices you make per stage regarding content and design.

3.9 CONCEPT CODE, THE MODEL

The next three chapters we describe how each stage of the concept emerges. We realise that, in contract to the dynamic character of concept thinking, this is a static approach. In order to best understand how each stage is constructed and what you need to do per stage to develop it, this static approach is the most effective. Therefore, do remember to constantly consider the working principles as mentioned above. Know where on the ladder your concept is located and what stage of the concept has become imbalanced by the trigger you have observed in the context. A concept is not complete until it has come to live and all necessary concept carriers have been implemented. You now also know the process of concept development is usually iterative. Therefore, we do not recognise phases, but elements. If you understand which stage has become

Figure 3.3 Elements Model Concept Code

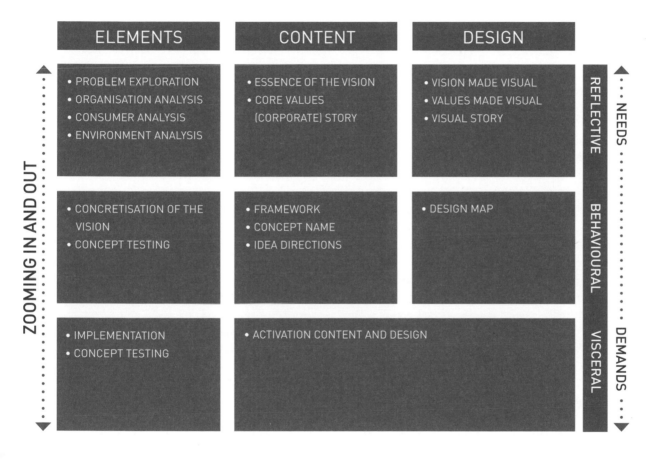

>>ALLOW YOURSELF TO WONDER. QUESTION EVERYTHING: WHY IS SOMETHING THE WAY IT IS?<< Mark Leurs, TBWA

imbalanced, you also know what elements must in any case be deployed in order to further develop the concept. Subsequently, it depends on your starting situation and the domain in which the concept is created what elements you do and do not use. Below is a visual representation of the elements of concept development. You can see that you need different elements at each stage of the development, and that the development of a dormant concept is a more extensive undertaking than the development of the awakening concept. Still, the stages of a concept are interlinked; they need each other. A living concept has no body without an awakening and dormant part. Indeed, the output of the dormant and awakening concept come together in the living concept. The elements of content and design are different per stage. The model displays the elements per stage. These are the same for content and design, but naturally they take on different shapes. In addition, it illustrates what the output of each stage is for both content and design. It is an ongoing process of formulation and visualisation going hand in hand, in order to translate this into a unique output later on.

3.10 CONCEPT DEVELOPER SECRETS

Your starting situation and all the elements are all good and well, but they are useless to you without the required characteristics of a good concept developer. On the basis of literature and many interviews with experts we made a selection of the required characteristics. We provide you with an overview of them.

>>IN EACH PHASE YOU NEED TO BE ABLE TO DEMONSTRATE WHERE YOU STAND AND YOU COMMUNICATE THIS WITH VISUALS. AT THE BEGINNING THOSE VISUALS ARE FLUID AND ABSTRACT, BUT THEY GRADUALLY BECOME MORE CONCRETE.<< Mark de Jong, Kossmann.dejong

>>GOOD CONCEPT DEVELOPERS ARE PEOPLE WHO ARE HIGHLY INQUISITIVE, HAVE A BROAD VISION, AND ARE GENERALISTS. THEY HAVE A BROAD RANGE OF INTERESTS AND DARE TO ALLOW THEIR INTUITION FREE REIN. "CANNOT" DOES NOT EXIST. THEY HAVE THE GIFT OF BEING ABLE TO CONVINCE OTHERS OF AN IDEA.<< Jan Rijkenberg, BSUR

A GOOD CONCEPT DEVELOPER:

- IS CURIOUS
- IS OPEN-MINDED
- HAS IMAGINATION
- HAS GUTS
- IS GOOD AT OBSERVING
- IS INTUITIVE/EMPATHIC
- SEES THE OVERALL PICTURE/CAN ZOOM IN AND OUT
- QUICKLY MAKES CONNECTIONS
- IS CONVINCING
- IS WELL ABLE TO PLACE HIM- OR HERSELF IN SOMEONE ELSE'S SHOES

Naturally, you cannot embody all of these characteristics; you can merely strive to. Still, you can train and challenge yourself to have more guts or sharpen your skills of observation. Can you learn concept thinking? We believe you can, with the sidenote that naturally some will have a greater talent for it than others. It is a way of thinking in which we make much more use of both our brain hemispheres. The next chapters of this book discuss per stage what the elements mean and where they lead. It provides you with a more concrete insight into how you can develop each stage of the concept. As you were able to read in chapter 1, we consider each stage of a concept as an activity that takes place within the creative industry. Depending on your style and expertise, you could therefore also be an expert in one stage of the concept.

DEVELOPMENT, THE DORMANT CONCEPT

DEVELOPMENT, THE DORMANT CONCEPT

In chapter 2 you were able to read that a concept consists of three stages: dormant, awakening and living. Even before you start with the development of the first stage, the dormant concept, you need to know what the trigger is for the start of the concept thinking process. This will always bring you back to the dormant concept. We therefore consider the dormant concept the essential stage for the success of your concept. The stronger your dormant concept, the more stamina your concept ultimately has. The importance of conducting thorough research and analysis is often underestimated in this. The research then remains superficial and generates too few insights, which eventually results in difficulties in activating the content and design in the living concept. After all, the dormant concept determines the choices made in the living concept. If your vision and your story do not sufficiently stand out, this automatically means that your concept carriers will not either.

Creativity is an important aspect within concept thinking. As mentioned above, the collaboration between the left and right brain hemisphere is essential to the successful creation of a concept. At first glance, the dormant concept rather seems reserved for our analytical brain, but nothing is farther from the truth. Here creativity also fulfils an important role: creativity starts before the creative starts. Earlier on, we recognised that on the one hand concept thinking takes the needs of the consumers and users as a starting point. On the other hand, new combinations are sought to arrive at products and services that have not yet been recognised as a need by the consumer. The road towards a perfect dormant concept is often long and conducting research thus requires a curious

perspective. In some cases the research phase of a concept can take up to a year or even years. This already points towards the importance of conducting solid research at this stage. There are many opportunities, but they will not come to you by themselves. You need to be your own engine, and steer yourself. This phase is particularly suitable for curious and self-willed people. At first glance, the phase seems reserved for the more analytical concept thinkers, but nothing is farther from the truth. This phase also benefits from your creative/intuitive brain. You need to be able to observe things very consciously with the use of all your senses. In this phase you demonstrate guts, search for the unknown, and look for a challenge in everything. Every situation and every subject can contain inspiration. In this phase you take notes, look for and take photos, collect things and eventually make connections. You need to be able to place all your loose thoughts into a framework. You observe, but need to be able to use this information in the right way and eventually arrive at an effective vision; the content output of the dormant concept. At the same time, you need to be occupied with seeking images to visualise facts and data to represent a feeling and an emotion. Here you think about reflective design, thus how you can apply design to tell your story. Design fulfils a symbolic function here. The entire dormant concept is an internal story, both the content and design component. You need this to make the right choices further down the line.

In this chapter we focus on the development of the dormant concept. If you have effectively covered all elements, you can determine the essence of the vision and the core values. Moreover, you can then write the (corporate) story. We refer to this as the content output of the dormant concept. These elements simultaneously lead to design output: vision and values in images and a visual story. We first describe the entire content component and subsequently the design component of the dormant concept. Do not forget that this is a static approach for a dynamic process. This therefore means that the implementation of the elements can differ. In chapter 7, we provide a number of suggestions for you to get started with. In the elaboration on the elements we in principle assume a situation in which you still need to create everything from scratch. Should this not be the case, for instance because you only need to work on concept enhancement, then you will still have to take a critical look at the elements to see whether you have implemented them in the right way. Here and there we add some nuance per different starting situation.

4.1 ELEMENTS OF THE DORMANT CONCEPT

Now that you know where the process of concept thinking began and where on the ladder the concept is located, you have arrived back to the dormant concept. The elements of the dormant concept for both content and design consist of successively: problem exploration, organisational analysis, analysis of consumer behaviour, and environment analysis. If you have thoroughly covered all elements of the dormant concept, you can describe the essence of your vision, the core values, and the story. We refer to this as the content output of the dormant concept. In addition, you can use those same elements to determine the design output of the dormant concept. This then provides you with the vision and values in image and visual story.

4.1.1 PROBLEM EXPLORATION

Problem exploration always occurs, although sometimes more extensively than others. Problem exploration is incredibly important. After all, you need to know exactly what you are starting with. In order to approach problems in the right way, it is necessary to look at the challenge from various standpoints. If concept thinking starts with a question, the briefing is important. You will receive this from your client. It will outline where the problem comes from, the objective, the target groups, the budget, and the preconditions. From the briefing you will further explore the problem. You walk around the problem area, so to speak, looking at it from various angles and formulating various definitions of the problem. Is the briefing clear? Is any information missing? You search for the objective, the background information, and the subproblems. It is important to have a good approach to this. Sometimes a problem seems the true problem to the client, but upon further exploration you might actually encounter a very different, underlying problem. Always look for the false bottom, the question behind the question. Or even better: look for the need behind the question. Focus on the 'why' behind the problem and in doing so try to reframe the original question. Indeed, framing is not about the truth of facts, but the appreciation of them. Start from a situation in which you personally have seen an opportunity or problem, as this will lead you to investigate this even further. Where does this opportunity or problem come from, what is your objective, who is your target group, what is your budget, and what are the preconditions? What are the trends and developments that are aligned with this? From this information you will further explore the problem or opportunity. It is important to not just sniff out the question, but also the underlying need. In this exploration the first contours become visible of your possible strategy. The problem and accompanying recognition provides direction to the kind of value creation to which you wish to respond as concept.

4.1.2 ORGANISATIONAL ANALYSIS

When you are dealing with a concept at a higher level, this means that there is already an organisational concept. You will then apply the element organisational analysis differently. You no longer just have to look for drivers, as they are already familiar, and recorded in the DNA. Consider the values and the vision of the company and make sure that your concept aligns with this. Search the core values: what makes this organisation different from the others? Who is the organisation really? Rob van Es (2008) writes that organisations contain upper currents and undercurrents. The upper current in an organisation is conscious, rational, and directive, and can be managed easily. It recognises a language in which business-economic and managerial thinking is reflected. The upper current consists of all attempts to manage the organisational processes rationally. It is about objectives, strategy, models, et cetera, meant to steer the organisation in a conscious manner. The undercurrent in an organisation is unconscious, irrational, and associative. It is about emotions, personal interests, experiences, desires, and relationships. It is the layer in an organisation that is not acknowledged officially and openly, but is there. They are the human aspects that cannot be directed rationally. If you start looking for who the organisation really is, you are also looking for the undercurrent of the organisation. The language that is usually spoken in organisations is the public language, the upper current. This is a language of opinions and analysis; sensitive and personal perspectives are not visible in this. That is actually the language that contains personal and professional doubts, the language of intuition and desires, the language that brings us closer to the essence of the organisation. In order to make this language visible, you will have to dive into the organisation and not just speak with the manager and/or the client. In order to be able to search for another language, that of the undercurrent, you can strike up a conversation on the basis of a rich picture (Coenen, 2005) or an image. In chapter 7, this is further elaborated on. If you want to bring the vision of the organisation to life, then this needs to be felt and experienced internally by everyone. If you are clear on the identity of the organisation, you also want to know how it communicates its identity internally and externally. In other words: how does the organisation present itself internally and externally? Does the organisation have a good reputation? What image does the world have of this brand? In order to come across as authentic and real, it is important that the identity and image of the organisation correspond to the extent possible. As a concept thinker you need to know all these things. If your concept does not fit the organisation, then you lose credibility. If you are dealing with an entirely new concept for a client, you need to seek out the drives of that client. Should you wish to develop your own new organisational concept, you obviously need to look at your own drives: what is your dream and what are your values? It is a process of observation in which you use all your senses. Observation and interpretation are important for gaining insight into the operation of an organisation.

4.1.3 CONSUMER ANALYSIS

It is important to know what the perspective, drives, media behaviour, and values of your target group are. You need that information to find alignment with your target group, so that you create something that truly 'fits'. What are the (latent) needs of the consumers in purchasing products and services? What is the perspective of the consumers? It is also important to analyse the media behaviour of the target group. Where and when media is applied has a great influence on the way in which your message will come across to the consumer. If you know this, you can respond to it with the communication of your concept. Consumers are often not able to indicate their own needs, which means you need to not only respond to what they say: you also need some sensitivity. You need to be able to sense the market and search for subjective experiences and perceptions of the consumer. Values are highly important in this, as we ascertained above in chapter 2. The purchasing behaviour of consumers is determined by the values he or she strives for. Therefore, it is important to ask who, what and when questions, but certainly also the why question. The latter in necessary for finding out the drives, preferences, needs, desires, and motives. You can do so by looking for consumer trends. These are trends that transcend the various industries. As a concept thinker you need to look at the needs of the consumer in the abstract sense. With your concept you respond to the visible, but also latent needs of the consumer. The consumer wants to give meaning to the concept. Giving meaning means: interpreting data by means of attributing personal values and function. The means-end chain model is a manner in which you can get insight into this. In chapter 7 this suggestion is further elaborated on. The consumer wonders what value it holds for him or her. In this element you collect information about the target groups in words and images. The needs and values of the consumer are usually not immediately visible, but they are expressed in behaviour. You describe what you see, but also illustrate this in visualisation. You can do so by creating a so-called average consumer or persona, which is a representation of the target group in words and images. A persona or average consumer is a fictional person that serves as a symbol for the target group. Please note: this element is not always applied by concept developers. Sometimes you do not work with a target group, but develop a concept purely on the basis of your own values. The group will then form itself around your concept. In this case we speak of follower groups.

Let us come back to the example of Schiphol from chapter 2. Schiphol has an international target group and that makes consumer analysis extraordinarily complicated. Responding to (un)conscious, future customer needs is therefore a challenge. Therefore, Schiphol has developed a method for this in which they take universal characteristics of the consumer, as well as the internal needs of the organisation, as their points of departure.

In their ambition to remain Europe's preferred airport, they aim to create unique passenger experiences in which people feel seen, understood, and cared for. This personal approach is written into their DNA and recently anchored in a new passenger experience method®, named Q-cepting.

Q-CEPTING

The term Q-cepting consists of a combination of the words Concepting and Q-thinking.

Concepting is essential for Schiphol when it comes to making their vision 'to compete & complete' visible and tangible to their passengers, and for managing their emotions. Q-thinking refers to a holistic approach towards not only customer needs, but also stakeholders, and business interests. Outside-in and inside-out. The name Q-thinking comes from the three Qs that are used to define a new concept: iQ, eQ and sQ. The rational iQ is about functions, facts, processes, etc. The emotional eQ is concerned with conscious and unconscious emotions of passengers and personal feelings. The technical and emotional (eQ) have

always been part of Schiphol's DNA, but the spiritual (sQ) is something new for the airport. SQ stands for the spiritual, social quotient and refers to meaning and creating personal balance. Furthermore, sQ focuses on managing the collective energy of passengers in a building where one can relax and recharge.

The method of Q-cepting contains five stages to go from inventing 'the big idea' to finally getting it physically realised.

Q-cepting was used to realise Schiphol's recent successful passenger concepts, such as Schiphol Security Service, Airport Toilet Spa, EcoChic busses, Holland Boulevard, and Airport Park. The method is currently being worked out in detail towards a shareable form.

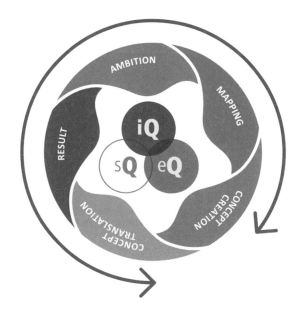

Source: Schiphol Group, M. Brouwer & L. Frijling (2015)

4.1.4 ENVIRONMENT ANALYSIS

Environment analysis can be done in various ways. Here we mean looking at the developments that are current in the market and industry for which you will be developing a new concept. What are those developments? What are the most important providers in your industry? It is also interesting to look at how others – your competitors – are doing in the market, outside of your own industry. If there is already a higher concept, then you focus on products that are already on the market, for instance. Try comparing products and/or services of the competitors for once. What do you notice? Within the market research you also consider developments in society. For instance, developments in the fields of politics and technology. The abolishment of the low VAT rate or other changes in legislation can be important for the development of your new concept. You also consider social trends and market trends in this. The social trends are located at mega trend level, in which social developments are mapped out. It is useful to look at this when you are developing a concept at a higher level of abstraction. After all, this is about developments in the longer term. These mega trends have a long-term character, but influence the needs of the consumer indirectly as well (Roothart & van der Pol, 2008). In addition to the mega trends, you also consider market trends. The changes that you notice here can provide insight into how you can develop a new concept that is located lower on the ladder, for instance. It can also mean that you make some adjustments to your living concept. Indeed, it is about the inventory of developments at industry level here. What innovations and introductions occur in competing markets? You could conduct trend research in an intuitive manner. Our society cannot be fragmented, seeing as there are not just linear trends that encompass the entire society. Trends manifest in signals. Thus it is about applying all your senses to pick up on those signals. Through our senses we gain knowledge of the world and of the changes in it. You visit locations that are relevant within the frame of your research and take notes, photos, and sound clips. You then search for the similarities within the signals that you have seen and can possibly make clusters. What is mutually supportive and what is contradictory? Subsequently, you give your clusters their own name and create your own trend. This trend you then visualise, briefly writing what the images represent and what they mean.

4.2 CONTENT OUTPUT OF THE DORMANT CONCEPT

The previous elements are necessary to shape your vision, your core values, and your core values and your (corporate) story. With the information you now have, you can make a rough description of the most important symbolic and distil the functional values from the analysis. You write the corporate story if you are working on a higher of lower concept. If a higher concept already exists, your new concept needs to be aligned with this. You then create a vision and story that are aligned with a higher concept. The concept at a lower level is aligned with the core values as formulated in the concept at a higher level. If no higher concept exists yet, you are entirely free to formulate a new vision on the basis of the previous elements.

4.2.1 ESSENCE OF THE VISION

You should now have ample material in words and images. The research part is behind you and you can now use the findings to describe a vision. The vision is constructed from two components: 'What do I see?' and 'What is my opinion on that?' In order to find that out, you critically consider your elements. A vision is therefore built up of an objective and a subjective component. The objective component is the factual part; that which you have seen, identified, and investigated.

With the details you have gathered from the elements you can answer the questions below:

....

WHAT ARE THE MOST IMPORTANT VALUES ACCORDING TO YOU OR YOUR CLIENT?
....

WHAT ARE THE MOST IMPORTANT TRENDS IN SOCIETY AT A CONSUMER LEVEL?
....

WHAT ARE THE MOST IMPORTANT DEVELOPMENTS IN THE MARKET?
....

WHAT DOES THE CONSUMER FIND IMPORTANT AND WHAT IS THE PERSPECTIVE OF THE TARGET GROUP?
....

HOW CAN THE TARGET GROUP BE REACHED?
....

On the basis of these findings you make a value fit, with which you make the analysis a bit more digestible. On the basis of this value fit you create your vision, thus form your opinion. Remember that the starting situation is decisive for the formulation of your vision. If you have a concept at a high level and thus an existing vision, hang this up on the wall. Never lose sight of this vision

in the development of the new vision. The value fit is a useful foundation for creating your vision. We therefore briefly zoom in on the principle of the value fit.

4.2.1.1 VALUE FIT

The DNA and values of the company and the consumer need to correspond. As we saw earlier, the symbolic value creation has become increasingly important: concepts stand out by virtue of their meaning. In order to be able to add meaning, the 'why' needs to be carefully considered. Consumers feel attracted to a brand on the basis of their personal values. Therefore, there must be a fit, a match between the company and the consumer. If you work on the basis of trends, there must be a fit between the company, the consumer and the trend. We call this the value fit. If you do not have a higher concept yet, a value fit needs to emerge between the trend, the consumer and the values of the (future) company. For a value fit you look at what similarities you see within the previous elements and then cluster these. You name the clusters and then select two, preferably even three clusters. This serves as the point of departure for the essence of your vision. You clearly explain the clusters. That way you have an overview of your entire analysis and can then start finding something in it, and form your own opinion. How you can go about this is further explained in chapter 7.

4.2.2 CORE VALUES

Determining the core values is difficult and vital at the same time. They are signposts for shaping your vision. This provides your strategy with direction and determines in what way you want to create meaning with your organisation – or underlying concept. The core values at the highest level of abstraction are generally fixed for a longer term. The concretion of this can vary and occurs later on in the awakening concept. At this stage – that of the dormant concept – you determine your core values on the basis of your analysis, in which the problem exploration offers direction. After all, this will clarify what the reason, need, and question is behind the concept to be developed. This also contains the core of the value creation. We advise you to limit yourself to four, maximum five, core values. In the development of a concept at a lower level, you select which of these core values will be represented in the concept. Core values serve as a bridge between the organisational and consumer identity, there where inside-out and outside-in come together, as described above in section 2.3. The values you choose are decisive for your strategy and therefore also for your choices in design. For instance, if you opt for impressive, symbolic values, the design will sooner reflect a certain modesty. In contrast, the expressive function will lead to visibility being more important. After all, you want to convey a story to others by means of the product/the service. The consumer values must also be aligned with the organisational values. The organisational values are based on the culture of the organisation; in the value fit various values per analysis component become visible. Depending on the essence of the problem exploration, you determine the selection of the core values. The value you wish to create is partly determined by the type of concept and the type of sector within the creative industry for which you are developing a concept. Expressive values, and thus for instance the perception value, will be higher with concepts in which the physical space in the living concept is the central focus. What we wish to emphasis with this is that in determining your values, you also need to consider where within the creative industry the concept to be developed is located and what value you ultimately wish to create with it.

4.2.3 (CORPORATE) STORY

Storytelling, you could write book on it. Concepts such as transmedia storytelling, social storytelling, interactive storytelling, and digital storytelling are all ways in which the (corporate) story can be distributed. Thus there is enough to elaborate on, but we opted not to do so in this book. However, it is important that you understand what a story does and why it is important within the principle of concept thinking. Depending on the starting situation of the dormant concept to be developed, you develop a corporate story or concept story for these elements. Every organisation benefits from having a corporate story. What is it exactly that you wish to say with your vision? For the concept story it makes a difference for which business sector within the creative industry you develop your concept. For instance, within immersive worlds the stories behind the concept are more essential in order to effectively be able to activate it in the living concept (the physical environment), while inside business services the story usually has a different function. Indeed, it is about strengthening the higher concept here. Let us get back to the corporate story for a moment, as this is the story with which the other stories to be developed must be aligned. The corporate story conveys the soul of the organisation, clarifying who you are, how you got there, and where you are heading. An organisation does not write or come up with a story, but the organisation is in itself a story. The success of a corporate story is largely dependent on the consensus within the organisation. The vision is the heart of the story of the organisation. Corporate story is not an objective in itself, but a means to get people involved in your organisation. After all, a good story is passed on, for instance because you are a proud employee. It is the living document and helps you visualise your vision. Activating the corporate story is letting new stories emerge that anchor the corporate story. This occurs with the concept stories. In all cases, try to make use of language that appeals to the imagination, let go of the control, and start looking for the undercurrent in the organisation. You can do so by for instance having everyone tell his or her personal story. Involve all stakeholders in developing your corporate story. You can elaborate on your story in a storyboard. You can do so making use of a persona or average customer. A commonly used method of development for this fictional character is making a story in comic strip form. The target group's experience of the concept is told and visualised in this. You can use this storyboard later on in the awakening concept, i.e. in the concept testing phase, in order to see whether your vision is aligned with the choices made in your awakening concept.

4.2.3.1 LAYERS IN STORIES

In some situations, stories are so complex that multiple narrative perspectives might offer a solution to maintain an overview of the complexity. There are situations imaginable in which you would want to address multiple target groups, such as a museum for instance. The content needs to be interesting for the connoisseur, but also be comprehensible for the layperson. This can be the case, for example, in the development of a new television programme for the whole family. A commercial focused on various target groups can then offer a solution. The separate stories must first be worked out, depending on the type of concept. Subsequently, the story can be worked out simultaneously or chronologically. For instance, an exhibition offers the opportunity to offer various aspects of the story simultaneously, while with a television format the story unfolds over time. Therefore, it is good to again consider your starting situation. An effective concept usually consists of at least three layers: a primary, a secondary and a tertiary layer. The primary layer is the first perspective, which is what we see happening. The secondary layer tells us just a bit more, and the tertiary layer conveys the deeper layer, the actual message. This is the layer of meaning. In order to be able to understand the meaning, the consumer will have to be able to process the primary and secondary layer. In chapter 6 we dive deeper into the processing, implementation, and activation of content and design.

>>USUALLY, THE TARGET GROUP IS BROAD, WHICH IS WHY YOU WILL OFTEN END UP AT A LAYERED PROPOSAL. THE FIRST LAYER IS THEN RECOGNISABLE AND ACCESSIBLE FOR EVERYONE.<< Mark de Jong, Kossmann.dejong

>>IMAGINE: YOU NEED TO SET UP AN EXHIBITION ON NAPOLEON. THINKING OF A METAPHOR CAN HELP HERE. IN THIS CASE, YOU MIGHT SAY THAT THE EXHIBITION IS ABOUT HEROISM. OF COURSE, THAT IS STILL QUITE ABSTRACT, BUT POWER IS ALREADY MUCH MORE INTERESTING. HOW WILL YOU VISUALISE POWER? THE METAPHOR IS AN IMPORTANT BUILDING BLOCK FOR US TO CREATE A SETTING THAT IS NOT TOO LITERAL.<<

Mark de Jong, Kossmann.dejong

4.3 DESIGN OUTPUT OF THE DORMANT CONCEPT

The elements of the dormant concept are vast in number and cost time. You constantly alternate between word and image, or rather between content and design. Design in this phase lays the foundation for fulfilling the symbolic function of design, later on in the living concept. After all, it is not until the living concept that the reflective aspect of design is perceivable to the end user. It is as it were the glue that connects the dormant concept with the other two stages. Design choices you make here in order to visualise your vision, story and values form the foundation of your future style choices and the manner in which you translate this into the content in the living concept. In this phase design is still fluid; they are atmospheric images and impressions that flow into each other and which get increasingly tangible on their way to the living concept. In addition, design helps to provide true meaning to the written word at this stage. People who think in terms and definitions observe the world around them from a different angle than those who think in images. In order to avoid confusion and contradiction later down the line, it is already important at this stage that there is a consensus on the meaning of the vision. Visualising the written word helps in this.

4.3.1 VISION MADE VISUAL

Now that you have described the essence of your vision in words, it is important to translate this to visualisation. Images can better convey atmosphere and feeling than words. It is important to get on the same page with the entire concept team and, if applicable, the client at the start of the concept development process. Do we mean the same? It regularly occurs that an image is sought, but that individually there still turns out to be a discrepancy in that which is meant with the vision. Images help to make this difference visible and jointly develop a sense for the vision. A mood board is a way to visualise the vision. In chapter 7, we further elaborate on the principle of a mood board.

4.3.2 VALUES MADE VISUAL

As we already concluded in chapter 2, values can influence behaviour and design is able to make these values perceptible. This enables design to influence behaviour. What goes for all design elements, also applies here: with design you make clear what you truly mean with the chosen core values. You look for consensus on the atmosphere and the emotion that should be experienced from the values. For instance, you can do so by searching an image that effectively reflects these values according to you. We regularly see that an organisation feels like they interpret the values in question similarly internally, until they start linking it to an image. This often leads to unpleasant surprises. Thus you search for consensus here, because when you have clarified this, it will help you make your core values more concrete in the awakening concept.

4.3.3 VISUAL STORY

In order to give more life to your (corporate) story, you need to personally step into the story as it were. See it in your imagination, as if you are experiencing it yourself, and then show what you are seeing. In doing so, use your full power of imagination and convert it into visual representation. For instance, make a storyboard.

This is then your visual story. What is the essence of the story? What are you actually saying, exactly? Take your vision as your point of departure in this. A good way to further develop this is by means of a metaphor. This is an important building block for shaping your story. Thinking in metaphors is highly practical in this. Through a metaphor you directly plant and image in the mind of the receiver. It is a tool for adding extra meaning to the language with which you speak with one another during the whole process – from the initial steps within the dormant concept up to the emergence of the living concept. The use of metaphors adds more coherence to loose components: they can break through existing thinking patterns and introduce another way of looking. In the creative industry metaphors are used in various business sectors. Examples of these sectors are the world of advertising, the visual arts, and exhibitions.

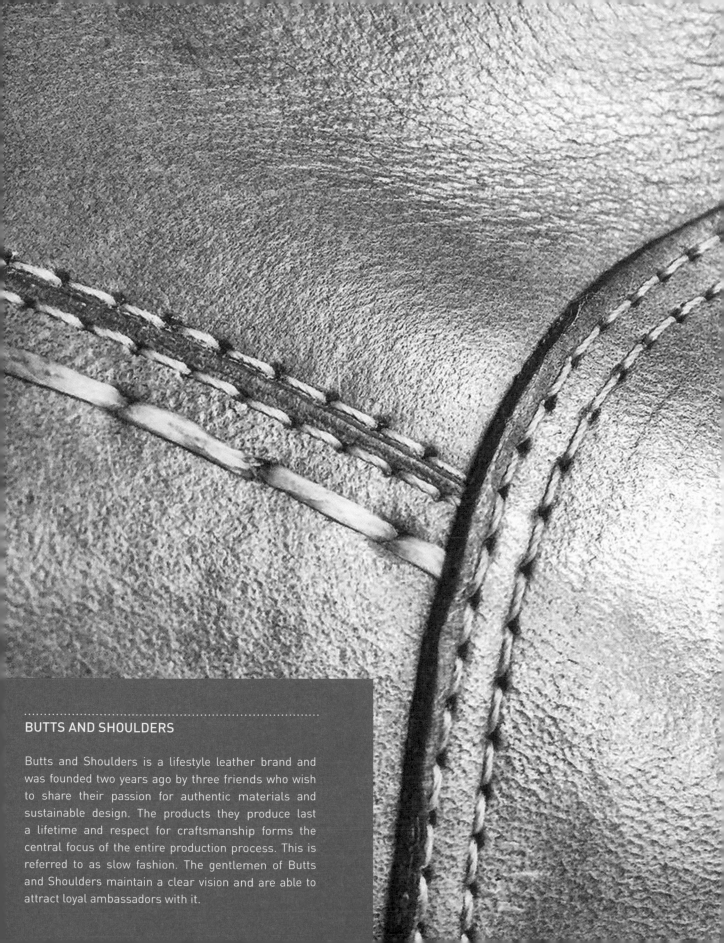

BUTTS AND SHOULDERS

Butts and Shoulders is a lifestyle leather brand and was founded two years ago by three friends who wish to share their passion for authentic materials and sustainable design. The products they produce last a lifetime and respect for craftsmanship forms the central focus of the entire production process. This is referred to as slow fashion. The gentlemen of Butts and Shoulders maintain a clear vision and are able to attract loyal ambassadors with it.

Butts and Shoulders is a lifestyle leather brand and was founded two years ago by three friends who wish to share their passion for authentic materials and sustainable design. The products they produce last a lifetime and respect for craftsmanship forms the central focus of the entire production process. This is referred to as slow fashion. The gentlemen of Butts and Shoulders maintain a clear vision and are able to attract loyal ambassadors with it.

CREATING ONLY THE BEST OF THE BEST

'We saw all the regular frameworks in fashion, and with frameworks I mean: you have your seasons, you have your collections, you have your retailers, etc. We wanted to challenge these regular formats. We believe that you ultimately become a puppet of the market if you keep up with the regular formats. If a fashion trend dictates that the new colour will be red and everyone then starts using red, then naturally it is commercially appealing to do that as well. But what does that say about your company, your vision? We started considering the origin of the products. What does the production chain look like? What kinds of actions are conducted in the process? We started looking for the real crafts, and in doing so it is always the objective to deliver the best quality for us. You would in principle always want to buy a product for the rest of your life. In other words, slow fashion. In this it is beautiful to see the product change with you. When it comes to leather, it is customary to work with chemicals, as this ensures that the leather does not discolour. However, we thought: what if you leave the product as it is, in its natural form? The only thing that is different then, is that it will discolour. And exactly that is what we wish to embrace. Indeed, the product needs to stay alive. In addition to our vision, we also have deepened a number of core values. One of these is craftsmanship and that already contains a unique element. We always want to collaborate with unique craftspeople. Moreover, we just do what we feel like ourselves. We need to get energy of it. Our naivety and fresh perspective ensure that we stay sharp and in this those collaborations with other craftspeople are so valuable. We really need each other to arrive at the best products. We want to be challenged. In addition, we never let ourselves be lead by what the market demands from us or by what rules impose on us. Storytelling is also important to us; it is a pleasant way of being able to spread our vision. We have recently converted this into a video (www.buttsandshoulders. com/movie/). We went to the factory where we witnessed people practise real craftsmanship, people that have been working there their entire lives.'

FRAMING,
THE AWAKENING
CONCEPT

FRAMING, THE AWAKENING CONCEPT

With your vision in your pocket you make the jump to the second stage of concept development: the awakening concept. This is an important, but certainly not a simple step. This phase is often underestimated and experienced as unnecessary, but the contrary is true. In the awakening phase, abstract terms and gathered information are given an increasingly concrete form. The activity central to this stage is 'framing'. In this stage, you give the abstract ideas from the dormant concept further meaning by connecting language to them. Coenen (2004) considers these 'linguistic' terms. The world is constructed by signifiers (words, definitions, and terms) of the language. You use this to actively frame meaning. Words, definitions, and terms are given meaning by the context in which they are used and the associations us people have with them. This meaning can differ in various cultures! Therefore, it is important to be conscious of the effect of language, both in the substantive context and the cultural context in which you use it. The vision is not a self-evident reality, it is a human construction. The symbolic value already lies hidden in the dormant concept, but is not yet concrete. By shaping it in the awakening concept by means of language, words, and images the vision can come into existence. This lays the foundation for the way in which the concept stands out and is expressed. The awakening concept is stuck between the dormant and living concept; it is a subjective in-between stage between these two concept stages. The awakening concept is an important stage because of two reasons. At this stage you provide your dormant concept with your action perspective. You do so by for instance making your core values and core qualities specific. You consider your strategy and the objectives of the concept, and this enables you to implement and activate the living concept. Secondly, the implementation of the awakening concept determines in what manner you will stand out in the market. At this stage, the foundation is laid for the behavioural function of design by considering the utilitarian/functional aspects. Your strategy is partly decisive for the shaping of your design. For instance, social design is a design method in which, rather than looking at what people want to have, what people need is considered. It provides new perspectives on current topics. The result does not necessarily have to be a product, but can for instance also be a service. You use content and design to develop your symbolic values.

At this stage of concept thinking it is increasingly clear that working with an interdisciplinary team is necessary. Entrepreneurship and creativity go hand in hand at this stage. It requires concept thinkers to be open for collaboration and a cross-border perspective beyond their own professional field. An entrepreneurial attitude and a great creative ability are necessary characteristics at this stage.

In this chapter we focus on framing of the awakening concept, in which framing could also mean reframing. This is solely applicable to an existing concept that needs to be given a new or complementary meaning due to a changing context. For instance, the emergence of technological development has ensured that we as consumers not only want to practice safe banking, but also quick banking. This leads to the need for reassessing how you shape your dormant concept. As soon as you have effectively covered all elements of the dormant concept, you can determine the framework and the accompanying type of business model, as well as the name of your concept. In addition, you have tested the first ideas and now bring the sharpened ideas with you into the living concept. You use the elements of the awakening concept together with the content output in order to shape your design output. In this stage, you shape your design in a design map consisting of various style elements, such as colour, typography, visuals, form, and material. The concept name is given a visual shape and is possibly supported with a logo. We first describe all elements of the awakening concept, then the content component, and finally the design component of the awakening concept.

5.1 ELEMENTS OF THE AWAKENING CONCEPT

The elements of the awakening concept are the con-cretion of the vision, the translation and concept testing, in which the final element is in principle the first overall feasibility analysis. All these elements serve as input for both the content and the design output. At this stage, in addition to the accompanying elements you also greatly need the elements and output of the dormant concept. Indeed, this is where the seed of your strategy lies, which you then further shape at this stage.

5.1.1 CONCRETISATION OF THE VISION

Now you know what the essence of your vision is, you know why you do what you do. If you wish to enter into a long-term relationship with the consumer through your concept, you need to implement your vision consistently in everything you do. We will get back to this in more detail later on in chapter 6. In order to be able to implement your vision you will need to concretise your vision, because otherwise your vision will remain an ideal image, an abstract mindset of which you are not sure how you will realise it. You have built the essence of your vision based on two components: 'What do I see?' and 'What is my opinion on that?' Moreover, you have summarised the 'What is my opinion on that?' in a statement that people can either agree or disagree with. This statement conveys in one sentence the 'why' behind your organisation/concept. That covers the dormant concept.

In the awakening concept a third component is added: you start wondering what you wish to do with it. By answering this, you concretise your vision. Making your vision concrete occurs in various manners. The manner in which depends on your type of concept and your starting situation. The most important components within this first part of concretising your vision are

>>THE VALUES WE ONCE HAD AS THE CITY OF EINDHOVEN, THEY USED TO APPLY FOR VIRTUALLY EVERY CITY IN THE NETHERLANDS. THAT WAS SOMETHING YOU COULD NOT STAND OUT IN.<< Peter Kentie, Eindhoven 365

>>YOU CAN ALSO APPROACH VALUES DIFFERENTLY. FOR INSTANCE, WE HAVE PILLARS: TECHNOLOGY, DESIGN, AND KNOWLEDGE. IF WE SHOW A HUNDRED PEOPLE THESE PILLARS AND ASK THEM WHAT CITY IT IS, GUARANTEED 95% WILL RECOGNISE EINDHOVEN. IF YOU ONLY MENTION TECHNOLOGY, THEN MANY WILL PROBABLY ALSO SAY DELFT, BUT THE THREE TOGETHER ABSOLUTELY SHAPE EINDHOVEN.<<

Peter Kentie, Eindhoven 365

the implementation of the core values, naming and working out the core qualities, and the tone of voice the communication with all stakeholders. In this way, you have named the 'why' (your vision and the elaboration of your core values) and the 'how' (core qualities and tone of voice). While implementing this you get busy with the 'what': the idea directions and of course the naming.

CORE VALUES

In the meantime, you have a (sharpened) vision and overall core values. It is now time to make those core values specific. In this manner, the core values are given meaning. This is necessary to be able to stand out. For instance, banks are often known for reliability and integrity, while fashion brands increasingly promote that they are socially responsible. This results

in organisations no longer being able to distinguish themselves and increasingly looking alike. That makes it more difficult to tell customers why exactly they should opt for that one bank. The way in which you implement these core values can vary. One thing does not have to exclude the other in this. For instance, you might focus on the identity value as a specific implementation of the type of symbolic value, but ultimately also increasing the perception value as a result. It might be that the demand has changed due to a change in the context. This is related to a change in demand that responds to the underlying need. For instance, the demand for a quicker banking method came from the consumer due to the emergence of technological development. This resulted in Internet banking. Let us revisit the example of FREITAG. One of the core values of FREITAG is 'intelligence'. If you do not add language to that, it cannot have any meaning and thus could apply to any company. What is intelligent according to FREITAG? They worded this as follows: "FREITAG keeps the future in mind: they act sustainably and reasonably. At the same time, we pursue innovation with ingenuity and playfulness". Playfulness is a big part of all their products and communication. They allow themselves the luxury of laughter. At themselves and at the challenges of life, in response to which they create products. Their humour is ironic to the point of being self-deprecating, but is never aggressive, hurtful, or fatalistic, sarcastic or cynical."

It is conceivable that your implementation of these core values will change due to developments in the future; for instance, that playfulness no longer is a trend and that this core value needs to find expression in some other way. How you make your values concrete also depends on your objectives and your strategy. What dimensions and value creation do you choose? This is possibly already determined in the dormant concept, as either the problem/question already provides direction to this or your analysis in the dormant concept clearly reveals this.

CORE QUALITIES

In addition to core values, the organisation has core qualities. These qualities are what the organisation excels in. You can consider these qualities as successes, the passions of an organisation. Core qualities come from inside of the organisation: they are part of the organisational culture. Core values and core qualities are closely connected. A difference is that core values provide direction to behaviour, while core qualities are more related to the skills and characteristics at which people within an organisation excel.

In the book *Competing for the Future* (1994) G. Hamel and C.K. Prahalad provide three criteria that a core quality must meet. These core qualities offer an organisation their competitive edge and must meet the following criteria:

>>COMPANIES USUALLY ALREADY HAVE A VISION, BUT IT MEANS NOTHING TO ANYONE. EVERYONE SHARES BLANK STARES. GROWING THE TREE… YES, NOW WHAT? IT IS IMPORTANT TO CONVERT THAT, WHICH WILL PROVIDE YOU WITH YOUR ACTION PERSPECTIVE.<< Marc Leurs, TWBA

BUTTS AND SHOULDERS

We believe our design can change the world. We would rather aim high and miss our goal, than aim low and reach it. We embrace our own foolishness and naivety, because it brings us to places no one has ever been before. It is this unpaved road that keeps us going. Leather is our core business. We touch it, we smell it. We respect it. Only the best is good enough. And we do not settle for less. Not only the hides themselves are important, but the entire process. From the design to the shelf, every step is relevant. And no matter how crazy it may sound, we think the cow deserves it. We do not follow trends or conform to markets. Our own vision is key. We work together with companies who believe in us. And with them we want to go the extra mile. We want to surprise. Overwhelm. Take on new challenges and prove that it can be done. We do not see our customers as cash cows, but as friends. Friends with the same attitude towards the world. Bold people, who had the balls to make a decision for the better. They use our products to carry out our shared vision. And together with them we will make up our own future as a family.

LEAD TO AN ADVANTAGE AND ALSO BE EXPERIENCED AS SUCH BY STAKEHOLDERS

BE HARD TO IMITATE FOR COMPETITORS

BE APPLICABLE FOR MULTIPLE PRODUCTS, SERVICES, AND MARKETS

We will revisit the elaboration of the framework in section 5.2.1 with an example of the Dutch supermarket Jumbo, which clearly demonstrates the difference between core values and core qualities.

TONE OF VOICE

The tone of voice is the style with which an organisation addresses its stakeholders. It is about the degree to which the character of your organisation is visible in the words you write and speak. It is not about what you say, but how you say it. What impression does it leave? What you say emerges from experiences and aspirations, and how you say it is shaped by your identity. If you separate 'tone' and 'voice', voice is literally the voice of the organisation. Your voice is inherent in your identity. However, your tone is something you adjust to the conversation.

You apply tone of voice in texts and other forms of communication. This consistency in language ensures recognisability and partly determines the image of an organisation. You could consider the organisation as a person. This person has unique external features, behaves in their own manner, and communicates in their own manner. The person serves as a model for the identity of an organisation with its values, core qualities, and features. This way it is easier to make

your own employees conscious of the identity and thus the tone of voice of the organisation. In addition, organisations can better brief external parties with the use of a persona. Because the tone-of-voice is made visual by means of the use of a persona, it is easier for people to understand. Depending on the situation or the person you communicate with, you change your tone: your 'voice' remains the same.

A tone of voice can be informal or rather formal, serious or light, direct or indirect, commercial or informative. In sum, the tone of voice expresses itself in many different ways. It is important that the tone of voice is used consistently in all communications by the organisation. For instance the website, flyers, and mailings. If you need to determine the tone of voice in the action plan for your developed (organisational) concept, you can ask yourself the following questions: How do values and core qualities influence that which you communicate as an organisation/concept? How can you bring expression to your core values and core qualities in the tone of voice? An example is the University of Leeds with their core value 'friendliness'. They translate this value to their tone of voice by bringing warmth into their words and communicating from the idea that they have a connection with people 'in a human way'.

We have just seen that you can make a vision tangible by specifying the core values, implementing the core qualities, and determining the tone of voice. You further expand the identity of the organisation. The second part of concretising your vision is more strategic in nature. You are going to link your objectives to your vision and determine where you 'want to be heading' as an organisation. These objectives offer a prelude to the strategy. For a strategy you think in the longer term. The objectives indicate where you want to be heading and the strategy demonstrates how you expect to do this. The strategy is a route that you map out and is focused on feasibility. You can see it as a mountain you wish to climb, for which you first need to make a plan in advance on how you will reach the summit.

5.1.2 TRANSLATION

The element translation forms an important bridge between the dormant and the living concept. Here you add concrete meaning to that which you have formulated and visualised at an abstract level, in the dormant concept. With this element you largely determine the direction of the living concept. Language, in word and image, is highly important in this element. By means of language the construct concept can 'exist' (Coenen, 2004). A construct is a way in which people create their own reality. In that sense you can thus say that concepts are in fact language. Language has inclusive or exclusive effect. In this perspective, language creates the reality of your concept; it creates meanings and therefore it also excludes meanings. You thus understand that in this phase you fix the meaning of the symbolic and functional value by making certain choices in language, but also in visuals. This translation results in a concept name, a design map, and idea directions for design. Idea directions are the first ideas. They can still be rough, but also more concretely on the product or service level. The practice indicates that these are already the first ideas for the concept carriers and that the living concept emerges from this. As mentioned earlier, concept thinking is iterative. The emergence of idea directions is a messy creative phase that results in the living concept, in which eventually

the shaping of the carriers takes place. These first idea directions are also called fuzzy front end, or phase 0: the starting point where opportunities are identified and ideas are developed even before the actual products and services are developed. In the creative process it is important to take the perspective of your strategy and take into account shifts as described in chapter 1. The outcome of the awakening concept is ultimately a concept, in both language and visuals, that is decisive for the implementation of concept carriers in the living concept. In addition, you also have the first idea directions for the shaping of your concept carriers.

5.1.2.1 SEEING, UNDERSTANDING AND GETTING CONVINCED

In order to be able to effective frame within the awakening concept, it is important to understand how visual language works. Let us introduce three theories to you that will help you convert the dormant concept in a way that does justice to the meaning that you ultimately wish to create. We wish to emphasise that this is not a design book and we therefore will not dive deep into each of the theories. We limit ourselves to that which we consider relevant for the concept thinking method.

Effective application of these three theories can ensure that the dormant concept is interpreted (Gestalt theory) in the correct manner and understood (semiotics), and that it convinces (rhetoric). We now describe this for the awakening concept, but these theories also apply to the living concept. Why is one thing clearer than another and why is this image more appealing that image? Furthermore, the laws of Gestalt can answer questions such as why we interpret on thing as foreground and the other thing as background. They explain the also often indicates in what direction we should seek the meaning of the sign. By combining signs with other signs they usually receive their most important meaning. Semiotics assumes that meanings are also largely constructed through contrasts. The word 'thick' only adds meaning because we know the word 'thin'. In addition to the sign being perceptible, it also invites interpretation. At this turn you also need to think about your target group again. For instance, not everyone knows that the pictogram below signifies a motorway. Sarah, Gaby's daughter, interpreted it as a picnic bench.

We can distinguish between various concept carriers, subdivided into iconic, indexical, and symbolic signs. An iconic sign is given meaning by means of similarity and is therefore easy to recognise. Sometimes this is partly culturally determined. Indexical signs create an association between the sign and the object. Symbolic signs create a connection between sign and object on the basis of agreement, which is learned. In this book, we will not further dive into this. You need to realise that people can only recognise the things they already know. You can only recognise that the red cross below belongs to the Red Cross organisation if you know this. In semiotics this is called 'denotation'. This is useful to keep in mind, for instance, when it comes to story layers. For instance, in Efteling (largest Dutch theme park) the park's mascot Pardoes is recognised as a jester (or maybe not even, if you are not familiar with the concept of 'jester') due to his red pointed shoes with bells. This is a prime example of denotation. At this level, the first layer, it is about matters such as form, size, material, colour, etc. Primary denotation is fixed: black is simply black. Secondary denotation depends on your knowledge of the world. Secondary denotation – in

the case of the theme park Efteling thus the reference to the mascot that serves to keep people's belief in fairy tales alive – can only be known once you have a bit more information.

The second layer of meaning is connotation, the emotional value. This is the appreciation of that which is perceptible on the grounds of shared or personal values. For concept thinking this is an important component, seeing as the interaction with the individual plays a big role in this. Whereas with shared values are about feelings of which you can presume that many people share them, at an individual level you add meaning to it yourself on the basis of your own context. Rhetoric helps you as a concept thinker and designer in order to be able to convince. For instance, why is bank A more reliable than bank B? With rhetoric you express your values a more convincingly. The various means of persuasion – ethos, pathos, and logos – offer an important insight in this. If you make use of ethos, you increase your credibility. We will explain this with the example of the banks. For banks, credibility and reliability are essential. For instance, you can choose to make use of credible ambassadors in order to increase you ethos. Pathos relates to responding to the emotions of your end users. Using image and design you can call on the feeling, with as the objective to convince them with the use of a certain message. In this it is not only about what is depicted, but also about how and especially what is not depicted. Finally, logos refers to the arguments with which we try to convince the end users. An example of the power of argumentation is for instance the use of the well-known 'before and after' photos. Drawings and images are also used to support argumentation. A sketch of a new attraction in a theme perception of visual communication. Semiotics tries to answer the question of how meaning is constructed and understood. Rhetoric refers to the power of persuasion of communication material. What moves us? As a concept thinker it is your job to solve problems as good as and as clearly possible. These theories also help you convey universal messages. As a concept thinker this might sometimes come in handy, for instance when you are faced with an international concept. Among other things, the Gestalt laws support the designer in this. Gestalt ensures order in visual communication for both makers and users. Of course, individual taste is always at play. This is also the case in design, but the Gestalt laws offer a better grasp of design. A number of simple laws ensure that we as end users can group a visual message. We have opted for explaining nine of them, which are relevant to design in this phase (van den Broek et al, 2010):

LAW OF FIGURE AND BACKGROUND; by separating fore- and background from each other, our perception is organised.
LAW OF SIMPLICITY; the well-known 'less is more' of German architect Ludwig Mies von der Rohe (1886-1968) still applies. It is one of the most important principles for creating use value, because it increases usability.
LAW OF PROXIMITY; this concerns the idea that when elements are located close together, the end user will interpret these as a group. Elements that are located far away from each other are perceived as being independent from each other.
LAW OF SIMILARITY; this is one of the most important Gestalt laws when it comes to concepting. A good concept is one coherent whole: you can see that

services and products belong together. You can create a coherent whole by effectively applying the law of similarity.
LAW OF SYMMETRY; our brains love symmetry. Symmetrical images are therefore experienced as a unity. Consciously breaking this law is a good thing, as it is a matter of taste and can actually ensure that the design stands out.
LAW OF SIMILAR BACKGROUND; this is an extension of the law of similarity. A similar background colour is one of the most effective ways to group objects.
LAW OF CLOSURE; our brain will complete an image. Even if you do not depict things, our brains will fill these gaps, so that a logical connection emerges after all.
LAW OF PAST EXPERIENCE; we tend to perceive, compare, and connect objects to things we already know.

The Gestalt laws provide order, and meaning that we then connect to that which we see can be explained by the theory of semiotics. Semiotics is the manner in which people provide meaning in a communicative situation. In the field of concept thinking this is important to realise, as it is indeed about creating meaning. For instance, are you occupied with designing a musical poster, you need to ask yourself how you can ensure that people will instantly understand that this poster is about a musical, even when it does not depict a musical. This is connected to the way in which people add meaning to it in a communicative situation. Elements that carry meaning are referred to as signs. Sound can also be a sign. Most of us now immediately recognise the sound of an incoming message or an incoming email on your iPhone. In order to understand a sign, we must know the 'code' and be informed about conventions (Van den Broek et al, 2010). The context park ensures that the consumer will feel convinced that they want to visit the attraction as soon as it is actually finished.

5.1.3 CONCEPT TESTING

It is difficult to estimate in advance how much symbolic value a concept will deliver. Stakeholders find it difficult or even impossible to assess the advantages of a concept before they have experienced it. We use the word stakeholders here, because we see that at this stage the focus is not only on the consumer. Only addressing the consumer is not sufficient, as you for instance also want to create consensus internally - within your organisation. The staff of the organisation also needs to live according to the concept: they must carry the concept, otherwise it is not credible. The employees are in the first place ambassadors of the concept and/ or the organisation. If an organisation pays attention to its employees in this way, the organisation flourishes and gets meaning for its employees. Performances and innovative capacities of the employees improve when organisations take their internal branding serious, according to Nicolas Ind in the book *Living the Brand* (2007).

A concept largely has few objective aspects on the basis of which it can be assessed. For that reason alone it is useful to also concern yourself with concept testing in this phase. In addition to applying concept testing in the awakening concept, you will also do so in the living concept. The two forms that we distinguish in this are pre-prototyping for the awakening concept and prototyping for the living concept. A pre-prototype is a more abstract form of a prototype. It therefore fits with the awakening concept in terms of level of abstraction.

Both are in this way immediately a feedback system. A pre-prototype can, depending on the concept, be a mood board, a business model, a scenario or a story-board. With a pre-prototype you hope to evoke reactions from your stakeholders regarding the first idea directions, names and choices made in typography, colour, material, and form. What does work and what does not yet work? You test at least three different idea directions with the use of the focal points of a strong concept. This testing is a cyclical process: you process the feedback and test again. You do this until you get no more new insights or responses. That's when your idea directions and design map are complete and you can incorporate them in the living concept. In the living concept you will further develop the chosen direction and then restart the concept testing.

5.2 CONTENT OUTPUT OF THE AWAKENING CONCEPT

The above-mentioned elements are necessary to shape your framework, your concept name, and your ultimate idea direction. The choice for the type of business model is also a part of the framework. We consider this important at this stage, which is why we will dive a bit deeper into this in this section. With the information you now have, you can make a rough description of your first idea for the living concept. You can further develop the strategy in a framework or you can, should the concept be located lower on the ladder, adjust the framework to concretisation, if there is reason to do so.

5.2.1 FRAMEWORK

In making a framework, keep realising the starting situation upon the start of the process. It is important that you only create a framework if there is not yet a concept at a higher level. If this already exists, there is probably also already a framework available with which the concept needs to be aligned at the lower levels. In the latter situation it might be the case that the trigger gives a reason to review the core values as expressed or adjust the objective. In other words: you adjust the concretisation of your vision. The framework is different for each company, but in order to support your vision you in any case need the core values, which you have made specific upon the concretisation of your vision. In addition, you consider the specific implementation of the type of symbolic value and connect objectives to this. An example of a framework is the case of the Dutch supermarket Jumbo. Jumbo applies the inside-out principle, placing the central focus on the customer at all times. They respond to the emotion of the customer and wish to achieve more in doing so than merely satisfied shoppers. They wish to be more than an ideal supermarket.

FRAMEWORK JUMBO

Essence of the vision of Jumbo: go beyond the point where others stop.

CORE VALUES OF JUMBO

Together; we have respect and attention for each other. We are open and honest towards each other. We work together and help each other when necessary.
Entrepreneurship; we see and seize opportunities, like taking initiative. We work with passion and drive, but also cost-consciously.
Winning; we want to be the best, put up a fight, and do

everything in our power to create real fans and realise objectives.

CORE QUALITIES OF JUMBO

Best service; we do everything in our power to ensure that customers go home 100% satisfied. Employees of the largest assortment; Jumbo considers it a challenge to go the ultimate distance. Everyone takes his or her own responsibility in this.
Customers can chose from no less than 32,000 different (brand) items at Jumbo. If they feel something is lacking, employees will ensure that the item in question is included in the assortment within two weeks.
Lowest price; Jumbo guarantees the lowest prices in the Netherlands.

OBJECTIVE

We wish to exceed expectations, every day, everywhere, and for each customer.

All of this has been converted into the 7 certainties by Jumbo, in which the above is reflected:

JUMBO'S 7 CERTAINTIES

1. Euros cheaper; customers always pay the lowest price at Jumbo. The price measurers check the prices in many supermarkets on a daily basis. If the customer finds the product cheaper somewhere else, then Jumbo adjusts the price. As a thank you for reporting, the customer also receives a product for free.
2. Service with a smile; the enthusiastic employees are always at the customer's service with expert advice or

for answering questions. And should the customer not be able to find a product, then they will come with you.

3. For all your groceries; with an assortment of 32,000 products, Jumbo has the largest assortment, from premium brands to cheap budget brands. And of course Jumbo's private label.

4. Fresh truly means fresh; al Jumbo we work with daily fresh products and specialists. Is the expiration date of a product today or tomorrow? Then the customer can bring the product home for free. The flowers have a 7-day vase guarantee.

5. Quick shopping; at Jumbo customers can do their groceries quickly and efficiently. Is a customer fourth in line and is there still a checkout counter available? The customer can then bring home their groceries for free.

6. Not satisfied? Money back guarantee!; customers who are not satisfied with one of the products, receive a replacement product for free or their money back.

7. Focus on your wishes; Jumbo can only be successful if the customer is satisfied. Complaints and comments from the customers provide Jumbo with the opportunity to perform even better every day.

5.2.1.1 TYPE OF BUSINESS MODEL

Creative institutions and companies alike benefit from an effective business model. The term 'business model' frequently arises in various articles, books, and conversations on the creative industry and several different definitions are used. The emphasis is largely placed on the sources of finance for the operation of the organisation. In our eyes, the business model actually forms a connection between the dormant concept, the strategy (awakening concept), and the living concept with which it is realised. A business model is thus not a static whole. The context and the changes that occur in it ensure the dynamic and possible adjustment of the business model. The advantages of the consumption of creative products and services are much more subjective and social in nature, which makes the business planning a lot more difficult (The Work Foundation, 2007). Building a business model around the commercialisation of symbolic value is then also a challenge. The demand for services and products are characterised by symbolic value is much harder to predict than products and services with solely a functional value. In all its simplicity, a business model describes how an organisation organises and activates value, and how it maintains its capacity to continue to do so. Not least, a business model indicates where the financial profit can be expected to come from. The point of departure in determining the type of business model emerges from your strategy. Cheng and Ludlow (2008) have made a clear distinction in three types. They call them 'social' business models. We gladly agree with this possibility, because these types of business models contain a form of social value and can therefore shape the symbolic value of a concept. We simply wish to illustrate that your business model is a logical result of your strategy and first idea directions, and that you as an organisation use this stage to think about this. If the concept to be developed is located lower on the ladder, the business model of the concept will be aligned with the type of model of your organisation.

Charity model: organise a business proposition that generates money and use the 'profit' partly or entirely for another activity that has social impact. For example, the Dutch National Postcode Lottery, a Dutch lottery founded to collect funds for charities.

Win-win model: organise a business proposition that has a positive social impact in itself. Organise in such a manner that there is a positive effect between the financial profit and the social profit – a bit of one and a bit of the other. The case of Schiphol in section 2.5 is an example of this.

Social Business Model: organise a business proposition that not only generates social impact, but simultaneously yields other forms of 'profit' as well, directly related to social and other forms of impact. Social entrepreneurship with for instance a social objective. The above-mentioned subdivision is characterised by the creation of identity value. From the perspective of the circular economy, Delft University of Technology (Bakker, in Creatieve Industrie in Beeld nl, 2015) has looked at various ways in which companies can create value in a circular economy. We highlight two examples that fit the principle of concept thinking.

Access model: in this model the consumer is not the owner of the product, bit is given access to the product and the accompanying service. The previously described example in chapter 3, Blendle, is a good example of this. The user gets access to articles in magazines and newspapers and pays a certain amount in exchange. Airbnb also falls under the access model. In this model access to and use of a product or service is the focal point. The economic value of this model emerges from the payment for that access. This model is aligned with the shift from owning to sharing.

Performance model: the product plays a subordinate role here. It is all about the quality of the service that is provided. Uber, which offers 'pay per ride' in an innovative manner, also falls under this performance model. A launderette offers 'pay per wash' instead of your own washing machine. This model is aligned with the aforementioned shift in order to respond to the emotional and functional needs of the consumer.

All previous business models express the shift from transaction to relation. This again underlines that it is becoming increasingly important to observe humans in order to eventually be able to achieve that meaningful experience. The format with which you can shape the type of business model is called the Busisness Model Canvas (BMC). The BMC offers a clear structure with which the desired information from the awakening concept can be organised and tested for feasibility. It is a form that you can use in addition to your concept direction in the concept-testing phase. In chapter 7 we will dive deeper into this.

5.2.2 CONCEPT NAME AND IDEA DIRECTIONS

For the development of the concept name a feel for language is important. The more powerful the name, the stronger your awakening concept. The name of the concept is the first thing the consumer will encounter. Also fall back on your consumer analysis for this; know whom you are developing for. What will your tone of voice be? Also take pronounceability, readability, and sound into account here. Especially if you are dealing with an international concept or if the concept might be expanded internationally in the future, the linguistic aspect is important. Never choose a name in isolation. Consider the role: is it meant as an organisational concept or as a product-service concept? Take the entire tone of voice into account. Also ensure that it can be integrated with design. The selection is often more difficult than the actual creation, so take ample time for interaction, for instance by means of co-creation and familiarisation. Moreover, do not loose sight of practical matters, such as technical criteria. For instance, domain name requirements and the countries and languages in which the name will be used.

Idea directions are, as discussed in section 5.1.2, the initial ideas you have for the living concept. We hereby again emphasise that you need to take your strategy as your point of departure and take the shifts in society into account. If you fail to do so, several ideas will emerge that do not fit the vision you came up with earlier. Of course, it is the intention that the idea directions for the living concept strengthen your dormant and awakening concept and that the whole of the three stages is consistent and coherent. In brainstorming for these idea directions, you start off with divergent thinking and come up with as many ideas as possible. You build on ideas and in doing so you fan out more and more, thinking of as many ideas as possible, until you have no more inspiration left. Then you start with the convergent approach. This is the bringing together of, making connections between, and structuring of all ideas. It is the act of bringing order to the chaos. The process of converging is more analytical in nature, because ideas need to be eliminated and the most powerful ideas need to remain. In this phase, you test the ideas by means of your dormant and awakening concept. The vision and core values are leading in this.

There are various brainstorm techniques for both the acts of diverging and converging. Many books have also been written on this. If you want to read more on this, then we also recommend *Six thinking heats* by Edward de Bono, *Creativity Today* by Igor Byttebier and the COCD Box methodology.

5.3 DESIGN OUTPUT OF THE AWAKENING CONCEPT

Design in the awakening phase lays the foundation for fulfilling the behavioural function of design later on in the living concept. It is in the living concept that this behavioural aspect of design is first made tangible to the end user, but in order to be able to realise this, the foundation is laid in the awakening concept. You consider how the functionality can been fulfilled by means of design and what interaction you wish to bring about. How can design come in to shape this? You can give the visual identity a form and this comes together on the design map. The choices are made on the basis of your strategy and the underlying symbolic and functional values. For instance, if you are dealing with impressive values, the design will rather reflect modesty. In contrast, expressive values will result in visibility being of great importance.

5.3.1 DESIGN MAP

A design map is the look and feel, or the visual identity, of the initial design direction that is aligned with the aforementioned idea direction. It can be described as the style of your concept. Style is a multi-sensory observation, a unique characteristic combination of style elements. In this, it is important that the individual elements are well aligned. Both taste, fragrance, form and later on also the product and service of the concept must form one harmonious whole, as described in the law of similarity. Style contributes to a high degree of recognition and capacity to stand out, but can also be used to convey a certain meaning (semiotics). Examples of these are 'modern', 'feminine', and 'cool'. A certain style can be a powerful point of distinction, provided it generates a positive consumer impression. If a style is related to the identity of the organisation, this style can only be understood at a reflective level by means of knowledge of the organisation (regarding its objectives, values, ideals, etc.) (Kootstra, 2006). In other words: when the appreciation, connotation, for a certain style is not only the result of an emotional attraction, but also of a positive evaluation of the meanings that this style represents, the value will increase. So, what exactly falls under style elements? This is a field in itself and, as mentioned, we are not writing a design book here. We will therefore not discuss all the details of graphic design, but focus here on the elements that we feel at least deserve attention in the awakening concept as we visualise it.

5.3.1.1 TYPOGRAPHY, COLOUR, VISUALS, SHAPE AND MATERIAL

• All letters have their own character. Choosing a font is therefore not easy. You need to feel good with a letter and that is a matter of taste. Typography is a tool in order to provide text with a visual character. You could consider it as the art or skill of handling letters. Typography is determined by the kind of text. For instance, you will use a different kind of typography for a newspaper than for a poster. A font will 'give away' your personality, but of course this also applies to the colour, shape and materials an organisation uses. Typography can make or break your design. The choice for the right font can make your message more attractive, readable, convincing and meaningful. Choosing the wrong font can have the reverse affect: it can damage your credibility or even leave your message unread. In your choice of typography you therefore need to take into account the design, the sector or the organisation for which your typography is meant. The typography needs to match the identity of an organisation or topic in terms of appearance. In your choice of typography, colour, shape, and material you can also refer to the theories from section 5.1.2.2. Following Gestalt (unity and simplicity), you limit yourself to one, two, and a maximum of three letter families. Semiotics also help you in making style choices. The M of McDonald's is recognised in the entire world. In making choices, be sure to keep it simple, as frivolity rather distracts than adds anything. Also carefully consider what channel you wish to use for this. After all, reading on the web is different than reading from paper. Therefore, not only consider your target group, but also your application.

• In addition to typography, you make choices in colour, too. In the Netherlands, milk chocolate is generally packaged in a blue wrapper and dark chocolate in a red wrapper. Tony's Chocolonely consciously deviated from this, because it wanted to be convincing (rhetoric) with its message. In 2005, they had a milk chocolate bar wrapped in a red wrapper. However, the general opinion was that a milk chocolate bar should be wrapped in blue. People called in angry to say they had done it wrong. This example underlines the function of design and the way in which you – in this case – apply rhetoric and semiotics. If we come back to colour, we can say that brown is a sombre colour and that blue is cool. What one person calls green-yellow, another calls green-grey. In order to still be able to convey your ideas, the colour industry has set up a standard. Colours are indicated with numbers and codes. As a designer, you apply a Pantone colour coding. This system is based on fifteen basic colours, each with their own name. Colour is a uniquely commercial product and can therefore also partly determine the economic value of the concept. This is visible in fields such as the fashion industry, in which colour agreements are made two years in advance on the basis of trends. Research also shows that people like blue and that applies for various cultures (Van den broek et al, 2010). However, when you start looking at the context and thus the application, making colour choices for the concept becomes more difficult again. The preference also alters depending on the context in which the colour needs to function. You can feel that black is a beautiful colour when it stands by itself, but as soon as an entire event is provided with black decoration, you will understand that this can evoke a different emotion. When it comes to focus, white is by far the best tool. In a society in which we are flooded with information, the power of white should not be underestimated. Thus, use colour purposefully. Will you opt for attention, atmosphere, or unity? Also take cultural meanings of colour into account. Of course, in this case it is again the target group that ultimately provides the meaning to it. However, some colour conventions are so ingrained into a culture that it is not advisable to deviate from them. If you wish to indicate that something is good or safe, you generally do this with the colour green. You will understand that it is not advisable to deviate from this.

• Visuals constitute stylistic elements that have become an indispensible part of our current zeitgeist. We work with the definition that a visual is a (photo) graphic representation of an idea, object, or area, in tangible or virtual form. Visuals can consist of both photography and illustrations. Visuals have the capacity to convey an idea or a large amount of information extremely quickly. This is why they play an important role in design. As we know, an image speaks a thousand words, and therefore it is crucial that organisations are highly selective when it comes to the visuals they use.
In the design map, visuals have the function of depicting what the world of the concept will look like, in addition to the typography, colours, shapes and materials. The visuals you as an organisation use must be a representation of your identity. What atmosphere do you wish to convey? What types of images best allow you to do this? How do you tell the story of your organisation through visuals? It is important that the visual identity is consistent in terms of the instruments that are used in all moments of contact with the consumer. Finally, it is vital that visuals and other stylistic elements mutually strengthen each other and form a whole together. All stylistic elements need to be applied across all expressions of the concept.

• Shape is also an important aspect within the design map. The shape also tells a story. The term shape can have meaning in various contexts. We are assuming shape to mean the external appearance of an object that takes up a space in its environment. This space can both be expressed in a three-dimensional and two-dimensional environment. Think of a square/cube, circle/sphere, rectangle/bar, and triangle/pyramid. You can see a shape due to its spatial limits. The properties of shapes are important within concept thinking, because they evoke emotions. For instance, consider shapes in terms of spatial or flat, simple or complex, geometrical or organic, and closed or open. Sharp and angular shapes can seem aggressive or actually radiate power, while round and wavy shapes come across as friendly and harmonious. Shape is used both on the flat surface (for instance in a corporate style) and spatial (for instance in the physical environment). When a person in a museum steps into a space with an organic sculpture at its centre, that provides an entirely different feeling than when that same space would contain a geometrical angular sculpture. This conveys a completely different story. This meaning of the shape within the story is also connected to the context of a space or world within the museum. Memory and recognition are important in this: we have associations with certain shapes. It is important to also show the visual language of a concept. This gives a clear direction for further implementation: it is expressed in your corporate style, but also in your concept carriers.

• In addition to colour, typography, visuals and shape, material also has a great influence on the atmosphere and appearance of your concept. Materials can carry out a message or evoke associations. If you want your concept to be aligned with the principle of circular economy, you will take this into account in your choice of materials. Cradle to cradle is a way to align with this. The design of a product needs to be fully reusable. You then use sustainable materials for this. It is not always easy to pinpoint what makes a material sustainable and this depends on many factors. Examples of these factors are the establishment and production of the material and the economic life span. In some cases, materials are also the tellers of stories: sometimes they have more to tell than you would expect at first glance and that can make materials highly suitable as storytellers. For instance, they carry a past with them. With the 'from truck to bag' concept of FREITAG, each bag tells its own story. They give the material a new destination with this, what they call 'recontextualising'. Another

example of a good choice of material that suits the idea of the concept is the situation of Butts and Shoulders. They only use truly authentic and natural, vegetally tanned leather. Their leather is one hundred per cent free from chemicals. This ensures that the leather stays alive and eventually wears and decolourises in a beautiful manner. In your choice of material you also take your dormant concept into account and accompanying core values. You will understand that for a core value as transparency the use of glass will be a more obvious choice than stone, or for flexibility you will rather opt for supple material than for rigid material. The choice of material can also contribute to the experience of a consumer. What feeling do you wish to trigger? The texture of the material contributes to this. After all, this allows the surface of the material to make a certain impression: the material feels a certain way to the touch and ensures a certain look. These are all important factors that contribute to the experience and appearance of the concept. In the awakening concept, you create a style palette that consists of colour, typography, shape and material. Again, realise that concept thinking is an iterative process: you test, adjust, and retest, until you have made the correct choices. The choices you make in this process, you will transfer to the living concept. In that stage, the choices made come together and the manifestations of your concept become perceptible to the senses. It could in fact mean that you will still make some adjustments in terms of colour and material at this stage: after all, it keeps going back and forth between the stages of a concept until it forms one aligned whole. In the coming chapter, we will dive deeper into this.

BUTTS AND SHOULDERS: THE NAME

'The Butts and Shoulders are the best parts of a hide, which is what we create our products from. It was the rebelliousness that immediately appealed to us, it is something weird. I do not think many brands would have dared to call their brand Butts and Shoulders. It felt right immediately, everyone agreed on that. The logo as it were represents the butts and the shoulders: the upper parts of the Os are the shoulders and the bottom parts represent the butt. Perhaps you need for imagination for this, but we did not mind that. In addition, it also resembles a sort of stamp that cows or cattle receive.'
– Dirk Hens, Butts and Shoulders.

ACTIVATION, THE LIVING CONCEPT

ACTIVATION, THE LIVING CONCEPT

The living concept makes the two earlier stages visible. In order to properly be able to process the content, it needs to at least be perceptible by the senses. In the living concept content and design come together and become one. In this stage the stakeholders encounter the manifestations, the concept carriers of the concept. These concept carriers can be very different due to the great diversity among various concepts. For instance, a fashion concept could have a fashion show as a manifestation, while a food concept could have a food truck or special menus as concept carriers. The domain within the creative industry for which the concept is meant largely determines the kind of manifestation. For instance, a concept for an amusement park will place more emphasis on the physical environment, while a new TV format perhaps focuses more on (transmedia) storytelling. Upon the implementation and activation you thus need to make many choices, as you are not done after having chosen the type of concept carrier! In fact, that is just the beginning: many design choices will still have to be made. The time for concept action has arrived. Merely making functional choices is not enough: you need to activate something that communicates, which is attractive and emotional, and which ensures interaction and dialogue with the consumer. The choice for functional content that expresses the communicative content is determined here. The method is then determined by implementation of the three design functions. Important questions immediately arise. For instance, how do you ensure that your concept starts living and that the consumer will experience it? And how will the experience become meaningful for the consumer?

In the living concept you will apply the framework you came up with before in the awakening concept. Thus, you ensure the concept comes to life. The implementation is first done internally and this is when you consider the right concept carriers. The activation of your concept occurs externally. The word activation already says it all: you start making the concept active. For this stage, we want to provide you with a number of questions you can ask yourself in making the choices you need to make in this phase:

DOES THIS CHOICE STRENGTHEN THE ESSENCE OF THE VISION?

DO I CONTRIBUTE TO THE CONCRETION OF THE VISION WITH THIS?

ARE MY CHOICES ALIGNED WITH THE WORDS AND IMAGES FROM THE PREVIOUS TWO STAGES?

If you can answer these questions with a yes, then consumers will better be able to experience your concept. If you had to answer no to one or both question(s), this means that you should not implement your idea, no matter how good it seems.

In this chapter we focus on the implementation and activation of the living concept. In other words: the phase in which the consumer interacts with the concept. It is the moment at which the consumer attributes value to values. During the implementation, you will investigate which touchpoints are relevant for the concept and what is emphasised at which design layers within each concept carrier. By means of prototyping you will also be applying concept testing again, so that the ultimate concept carriers fit within the chosen touchpoints of the concept. The output of the living concept is therefore the activation in content and design. This output is based on the previous two stages, so also keep zooming in and out here. As mentioned before, content and design come together in this phase and become perceptible to the senses. Finally, we will briefly deal with concept monitoring and effect measurement of the concept in this chapter.

6.1 ELEMENTS OF THE LIVING CONCEPT

The elements in the living concept consist of implementation and concept testing. The implementation consists of two aspects:

• Your design map and concept name need to be implemented in all your internal processes. In order to implement something internally, you shape the concept carrier that is your organisation. The concept carrier organisation is thus always analysed and, where necessary, improved. If the concept is not alive internally, it has less chance of succeeding externally. A mentioned in chapter 3, the employees are the ambassadors of the brand/organisation. You can also use the customer journey map for this, but instead of looking at the customer, but at the employees of an organisation. This is also called the employee journey. As an organisation you can only realise a great customer experience if this is also translated to the employee journey.

• You need to choose the right content channels (touchpoints within the concept carriers), in order to shape your earlier made design choices externally through this content. In order to be able to determine this properly, you will also spend this stage on testing the concept. Depending on the type of concept and your resources, you do this by means of prototyping.

6.1.1 IMPLEMENTATION

In element implementation it is important to test your choices on the basis of the essence and concretisation of the vision and your design map. In order to test your choice on the basis of this, you must of course know how you make the right choices and what to look out for. It is difficult to implement the concept carriers in the right way. Every vision is different and you cannot transfer the implementation of the carriers from another concept one-to-one. In this case, it also remains important to test it on the basis of the client, the target group, and the remaining context. All individual concept carriers need to be aligned in terms of design and fit in with your vision. That makes a consistent whole. Be sure to take the type of concept into account. The more tangible your concept is, the fewer concept carriers you can implement in the living concept. You should never lose sight of the coherence between the components, it needs to be an interconnected whole. In chapter 2 you were able to read that there we can distinguish various concept carriers. In some cases these overlap. Let us freshen up your memory and immediately add the meaning to the carriers. As mentioned, the carriers largely overlap, too. A physical environment also communicates and packaging is both a product and a means of communication. We therefore purely list the six carriers in order to give you some direction and consider it less important to provide a framework.

PRODUCT; a product is a tangible good and is made or emerges. In concept thinking you can think of the following examples: gadgets, food, an event and packaging. This is just a small selection from the many different kinds of products.

SERVICE; a service is a non-physical good. A service needs to be purchased at the moment of production. For instance, customer service at Ikea or the food in a restaurant.

ORGANISATION; a concept has influence on the internal organisation. It can be leading for the culture and the behaviour within the organisation, the staff hiring policy, and internal communication and processes. The first component of implementation is the implementation of the logo and the design map in internal processes. The personnel first need to live your concept before you can activate the concept externally.

COMMUNICATION; there are many various ways and means of communicating from the concept. After all, you communicate both internally and externally. You exchange information and that information can be shared by various means. For instance, a website, newsletter, poster, comic, brand book or corporate style manual.

PHYSICAL ENVIRONMENT; the physical environment is the external appearance of your environment. Atmosphere, style, material, shapes, and colours are greatly important in this. You can use this to shape the world of your concept.

NETWORK; the network around your concept consists of various stakeholders. These stakeholders can be co-producers, suppliers, consumers and companies.

In order to determine what carriers to use, you need to consider the possible story layers in the concept (see section 4.2.3.1). What stories would you like to tell where? These layers co-determine the choices in content and design. It is important that in doing so, you continue to keep the output of the previous stages in sight. This means that in making the choices for the right content and the application of design you take into account the context in which the concept is activated. Je know your target group, are aware of the developments, and know within what domain of the creative industry you will be activating the concept. With this in back of your mind you start making choices for content. The previously made content and design choices are made concrete at this stage. The manner in which the content is processed determines the extent to which the consumer experiences it as a meaningful experience. The method of concept thinking assumes that you want to offer the consumer a meaningful experience. The previous two stages have been shaped on the basis of this principle. You know what ideas you wish to realise and what kind of symbolic value these ideas support. The implementation of the concept will therefore have to fit with the essence of your vision on the one hand, and will have to meet the demand and underlying needs of the consumer on the other. What content you use also depends on the functional values, the demand behind the need of the consumer. That means that you look at both the functional and the communicative side of content. In adding a utility, a feature based on the functional values, the newest technologies are often used. In order to make good choices for content and design you make use of the touchpoint analysis, create story layers for content, and shape the design layer model for the design. In this way you shape the experience in such a manner that it gets meaning. At this stage, you are occupied with experience design, as we have already described in chapter 1.

6.1.1.1 TOUCHPOINT ANALYSIS

Touchpoints are all moments at which the consumer encounters the concept. This can be direct and indirect. At these moments the consumer has a certain experience that influences his or her overall perception of the concept. Touchpoints are specific effects of a concept carrier. Touchpoints are moments at which a person and an organisation/concept meet. The consumer experiences the concept carriers before, during, or after the moment of contact in a certain manner (pre-exposure, exposure and post-exposure). As an organisation, you want to positively influence this experience in order to enter into a durable relationship. In order to be able to do this well it is useful to analyse the touchpoints, to map them. Only if you do so, will you know which carriers you need to improve or shape. It is important to ask yourself various questions. What touchpoints contribute to a positive customer experience? Which ones do not? Are the touchpoints developed in order to meet the consumer needs? Do all touchpoints deliver a consistent consumer experience? Is the on- and offline consumer experience identical? Are there touchpoints at which consumers disconnect? Why?

A way to get clear on the touchpoints of your concept is to make a customer journey map. A customer journey map makes the entire 'consumer journey' visual. Customer journey mapping is a way in which it becomes visible what content is important for the consumer. This map surveys takes the perspective of the stakeholder to consider the contact moments with the organisation. This is one highly effective and simple manner to visualise the experience of the consumer. It helps to provide insight into the sore points and moments of happiness, but also to improve the existing touchpoints. If you know where, when and how people come into contact with the concept, you can then improve the sore points. A proper analysis of all touchpoints provides insight into what concept carriers you will use for your concept or which need to be improved. In this it is important that you name all customer touchpoints; what concept carrier they belong to is less relevant, as the carriers often overlap anyway. The consumer should experience the identity of the organisation in an ideal customer journey. A check-up question in this is: if the name of the organisation was not mentioned anywhere, would you then know that this came from that organisation? If an organisation has a strong identity that is reflected in all concept carriers, you would have to receive a yes to that question. This is what we strive for in shaping (the improved) customer journey, the story layers, and subsequently the design layers.

For instance, if you walk through a store in your customer journey, you will encounter all sorts of touchpoints. Before they visit a shop, consumers already have an image of the shop. They have seen the social media messages and visited the website, and therefore have a clear expectation and image. Once they have arrived at the shop, the first thing the consumer will see is the facade. Then the consumer will look at the shop window and walk in. It is important that the shop confirms or exceeds the feeling the consumer had in advance. The consumer makes their round through the shop, looks at all the products, enjoys the interior of the shop, talks with the staff member, purchases something and ultimately takes home the brand brochure. In the shop the actual 'embracing' takes place. The overall atmosphere of the brand prevails and the ideas that the consumer had at home on the sofa are now being realised. This example also demonstrates that the concept carriers overlap. It is therefore highly important for the concept thinker to stick to the common thread for every link within the customer journey that he or she designs. Each step in the customer journey provides the consumer with positive confirmation in the choices he or she is about the make. The consumer is fully guided in this. Only in this way can the customer journey offer a smooth progression and connect the organisation/brand and the consumer with each other. The objective is that the connection with the consumer becomes increasingly close and personal during the customer journey. Of course, a prerequisite for this is that the organisation keeps conveying relevant messages and being transparent and authentic. If the organisation/brand does this well, the consumer will also assess this as a strong brand.

6.1.1.2 DESIGN LAYERS

The concept carriers each offer a specific design, and each type of design offers various layers. Together they fulfil the three functions of design as discussed in chapter 3: visceral, behavioural, and reflective design. These three functions need each other to make the design successful. Wally Olins (*On brand*, 2004) has subdivided design into various disciplines. We have linked this subdivision to our concept carriers, in which the relevant design 'network' is left out of consideration.

The subdivision of the concept carriers on the basis of the disciplines by Wally Olins (2004) is as follows:

PRODUCT DESIGN; this is about the physical product the end user encounters. As a designer it is a challenge to represent the symbolic and functional values in the product. The functional values are the minimum expectations the consumer has, such as for instance the technical quality or convenience.

COMMUNICATION DESIGN; communication design is controllable and is focused on finding solutions for transferring information. Within communication design you usually work from a message of story. Various disciplines within communication design are graphic design, information design, corporate design, brand design and web design.

> **>>DESIGN WOULD NOT EXIST WITHOUT THE FIRST TWO STAGES OF CONCEPT DEVELOPMENT.<<** Malika Favre

>>WE WANT TO MAKE BEAUTIFUL PRODUCTS. WE LOVE FUNCTION, WE LOVE THE SECOND 'WHY', WE LOVE THE LITTLE HIDDEN FUNCTION WHICH IS DISCOVERED LATER ON.<< Daniel Freitag, Freitag

ENVIRONMENT DESIGN; in this book we focus on the spatial design of both interiors and exteriors. For instance shop interior, museum interior, fun parks, restaurants and cafés. We do not take landscape architecture and architecture into consideration. Within environment design worlds are created in which every nook and cranny has been thought of. These worlds can be small or large. The most important is that worlds are created in which people want to be. Environment design can be both actual and virtual. For instance, for Bol.com the website is its sales environment and for an amusement park the park and the attractions themselves are.

SERVICE DESIGN; service design is about designing effective, efficient and useful service experiences. In service design it is not only about the service itself, but indeed also about everything around it. Service design is the bringing together of all touchpoints into one whole. The ultimate consumer experience is the central focus in this.

INTERACTION DESIGN; interaction design is the design of products and services in a way that they are suitable for use, easy to use, and allow people to enjoy the use of these products and services. The shape interaction

design takes can vary. It can relate to the use of household equipment, the ATM, the taxi company, the computer, the software programmes and mobile devices. What all these things have in common is that they serve to connect the user to the products he or she uses.

Perhaps it is needless to say, but of course the disciplines overlap in some areas. This makes sense, as we were able to conclude the same for the concept carriers. Within these design disciplines all design functions are represented. There is a difference in the degree to which this occurs. For instance, you will notice that especially the reflective function does not appear clearly in all disciplines. An example of this is that in communication design the reflective function is (almost) always present; in product design there is still much progress to be made in this area. After all, products are mainly based on the appearance (visceral) and the functional aspects (behavioural). By thinking about the story the product should convey, you can trigger your consumer from a reflective function leading to the consumer feeling more involved and intellectually stimulated. Of course, this is not important for all products, as some products only need the visceral and behavioural function of design.

The design layer model 6.1 has the objective of bringing the concept to life in a holistic manner by means of design. This model assumes the philosophy that when you wish to activate a concept and thus make it perceptible to the senses, you do not only consider the aesthetic aspects of design. The model offers various layers: for each concept carrier or even every touchpoint of the concept you look at all layers of design. It immediately offers a moment of assessment at which you can see whether the reflective and behavioural functions of design have been sufficiently thought out yet in the dormant and awakening concept. It is as it were a cumulative design process, in which the reflective design in the dormant concept forms the basis for behavioural design. Both functions of design become perceptible to the senses (visceral design) in the living concept. As mentioned earlier, there can be a difference in effect per concept carrier. This difference is determined by three factors that determine the coherence and effect of all stages of the concept. These factors are the starting situation, the place on the concept ladder, and the type of domain within the creative industry. In other words: the context in which the concept will be activated.

Figure 6.1 The Design Layer Model

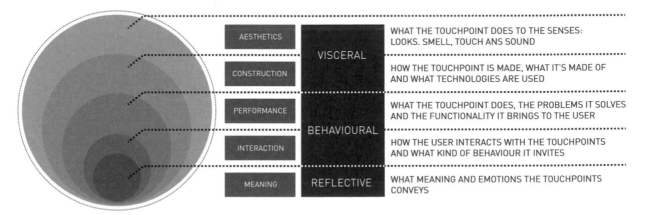

Source: Based on Brand Driven Innovation (2010)

SNASK

We will take a design example of Snask. Snask described itself as 'an internationally renowned creative agency that makes kick-ass design'. We had the privilege to be able to interview Fredrik Öst from Snask at their office in Stockholm. A beautiful example of SNASK's work is what they achieved for the Malmö festival in 2014. The three functions of design are clearly represented in this case. In 2014, Scandinavia's biggest city festival celebrated its thirtieth year of organising its festivities. This event took place in August and attracted about 1.4 million visitors over a period of eight days. Snask thought about the identity of the festival and wanted the Malmö festival to celebrate in style. To this end, they made the largest graphic identity that had ever been made worldwide: a gigantic physical artwork of thirteen by eight meters (reflective design). This resulted in interaction with the visitors. They could jump, climb or simply sit and relax on the artwork (behavioural design). In addition, Snask is always occupied with creating unique designs that cannot be copied, and which have not yet been offered in that way before anywhere in the world. It either appeals to you or it does not, but it is always a fit with Snask (visceral design).

6.1.2 PROCESSING

In order to create a meaningful experience the content of your concept needs to be processed. The manner in which content is processed determines the intensity of the experience. In order to be able to process content, we circle back to chapter 2, the individual values of consumers. Now that you have determined which concept carriers and which design layers to apply, you need to consider how those are processed before you move on to activation. The intensity with which content is observed and processed determines the power of the experience. In the previous chapter, we already saw that this is partly determined by the way in which our brain functions, attributes meaning to certain things, and can be convinced of a certain message (Gestalt, semiotics, and rhetoric). In addition, chapter 2 demonstrates that the individual value is determined by the way in which

MALMÖ
FESTIVALEN

16-23
Augusti

Gratis för alla!

Lemonad vagnen!

MALMÖ
FESTIVALEN
MUSIK · KULTUR
KONST & DESIGN
BARN · SPORT &
LIVSSTIL · MAT
& DRYCK · ❤

Läs mer om festivalen och programmet
på min nya hemsida → WWW.MALMOFESTIVALEN.SE

Scandic    Malmö stad

>>WE STRIVE TO CHALLENGE THE INDUSTRY BY DOING THINGS DIFFERENTLY. WE WORSHIP UNCONVENTIONAL IDEAS, CHARMING SMILES AND REAL EMOTIONS. WE SEE THE OLD CONSERVATIVE WORLD AS EXTREMELY TEDIOUS AND AS OUR BIGGEST ENEMY.<<

the concept is processed. This refers to the possible effects, emotions, and cognition that the concept can spark in the individual. In other words: the manner in which the individual acknowledges and perceives the experience. This is connected to the ability of a consumer to process the content. In order to be able to see and understand the various layers in a story, more knowledge and insight is required than to understand simpler stories that merely consist of the basic primary story. You will have to take this into account in making your choices. Competence is a decisive factor for the processing of the concept and thus also for the success of the concept.

When it comes to processing information, competence – or indeed Ability – is one of the three preconditions that need to be met according to the MAO model (Raaij & van Antonides, 2002). The MAO model is a much-used information processing model that you can also apply to the processing of a concept. The willingness to process a story or message is another important precondition if you want the concept to reach the end user at all. The consumer's willingness strongly depends on the motivation and involvement of the consumer with the concept. Consumers with a high sense of engagement are highly motivated to explore the entire story throughout all of its layers. A third precondition is the opportunity to be able to process the story of the concept. These three principles together form the MAO model: Motivation, Ability, and Opportunity. Motivation and ability are personal factors, while opportunity is a contextual factor. Depending on the type of concept, you can influence the factor of opportunity. For instance, external events can distract the consumer. The speed at which information is offered also determines what opportunity there is to process.

6.1.3 CONCEPT TESTING

The concept testing in this phase usually occurs by means of a prototype. A prototype is, as described earlier, more tangible than a pre-prototype. A prototype in the living concept is again directly a feedback system. In addition, a prototype can have multiple forms, depending on the domain in which the concept is located. A number of examples of prototypes are mood boards, concept books, scale models, representative models, simulations and scenarios, and role-plays or try-outs in case of a non-tangible product. If we link the prototypes to the concept carriers, a try-out would be a suitable prototype for a service in which real consumers are observed. For instance, this can be done by means of placing a video camera and analysing the footage afterwards. In case of a product (for instance an event) a scale model can be developed, so that a mini-experience is created in advance. This can be tested by a group of visitors. For instance, you can also come up with various prototypes for the physical environment, the network, the communication, and the organisation. The focus here is the feedback from your stakeholders. Get creative in thinking of ways to best collect this feedback. It is important that the stakeholders are able to connect to the concept and that your prototype immerses them in it, as it were.

As you will have noticed, the appearances of a pre-prototype and a prototype are often similar. The most important difference is that with a pre-prototype there is no or hardly any investment being made in the eventual design. This is why the pre-prototyping phase makes more extensive use of mood boards, storyboards, and drawn-up business models, because these forms hardly require any investment. The most important component of concept testing – which is not dependent on the awakening or living phase – is that it is mainly concerned with the interaction, the dialogue with the users in order to generate feedback in this manner. What works? What does not yet work? As soon as this has been completed, you go back to the analysis of the dormant concept. Does it still fit? Are you overlooking anything? Have you implemented all the previously made choices or do you need to review your choices on the basis of the feedback? You mainly use the concept testing for improving where necessary. All feedback on the basis of the prototypes (in whatever form) is seen as a point of departure for further development. The design can be 'built' in reality and be made operational within the given preconditions, technology, timeframe and budget.

IKEA KITCHEN 2015

A good example of prototyping is Ikea's design of the kitchen of 2025. Ikea wanted to find answers to the following question: 'What will kitchens be like a decade from now?'

Together with IDEO (an award-winning global design firm), students from Lund University and the Eindhoven University of Technology they developed multiple concept carriers on the basis of the vision ('Inspire creative handling of food and fighting food waste'). The world is changing and with it the needs of consumers as well. Students conducted elaborate research into these needs and this ultimately lead to the concept carriers we will be discussing here. Usually, research is preceded by prototypes that can be presented on a screen, such as a concept video or a rendering. IDEO went a step further: four concept carriers emerged from this collaboration, of which 'live' prototypes were exhibited at the EXPO Milano during a six-month exhibition.

'Modern Pantry' is a new way of storage which takes the principle of the visibility of stock: you need to be able to see what you have in your pantry, so that you can use its contents creatively and ensure that nothing exceeds its expiration date. 'Mindful Sink' tackles water usage and demonstrates how you can reuse water for instance in the dishwasher. 'Thoughtful disposal' deals with responsible waste processing and demonstrates how this can be done alternatively. Finally, there was also a concept carrier called 'Table for Living', which is a table suitable for cooking, eating and working due to the use of induction hobs. There is a camera mounted over the table which recognises your ingredients and provides you with recipes including everything you already have in your cupboard. In addition, the table give cooking instructions on how to prepare the recipes and combines tastes. IDEO has made several prototypes for Ikea. They started out in the studio with 1:1 polystyrene scale models of which the interactive table top was filled with cut-out drawings. They call this 'Low-resolution prototypes'. These scale models immediately provided an idea of what would later be turned into a working prototype. By means of storytelling and a persona, the kitchen was tested and then improved. In the follow-up phase the objective was to get the kitchen 'working'. A rendering was made and ten weeks were reserved for the 'real-life' building of the working prototypes. In other words: the 'High-resolution prototypes'. In addition to the materials for the kitchen itself, the technology for the 'Table for Living' came into play as well. Scenarios for use were thought out. The exhibition in Milan was the place to test these prototypes and see how consumers would respond to them. During the exhibition, it became clear that the scenarios did not suffice: the elaborated scenarios did not feel natural to everyone. For instance, people placed the vegetables on the table top in a different manner, due to which the technology did not entirely work. This revealed that the technology had to be reassessed. All in all, Ikea will incorporate the conclusions from this exhibition in its product design for the future. More information on this concept can be found at: www.conceptkitchen2025. com.

6.2 ACTIVATION

Activation is literally the process of making operative. This occurs by bringing your end users into contact with your concept carriers. Products and services of the concept are purchased by consumers because they evoke meaning for them. On basis of that an interaction with the concept emerges and the consumer either does or does not attribute value. During the application of your chosen content and design you operate on the idea that you strive for simplicity and enrichment in the entire customer journey. After all, the modern consumer is looking for complicity and at the same time wants an experience. However, due to the influence of the offering we encounter, this experience does need to constitute an enrichment for the consumer. In order to be able to achieve this, you fall back on your dormant and awakening concept. You try and discover the latent needs of the consumer in order to be able to respond

>>OUR THINKING IS ALWAYS STRONGLY INFLUENCED BY LAYERS. THE FIRST LAYER NEEDS TO BE ACCESSIBLE TO EVERYONE WITHIN A BROAD TARGET GROUP. THIS IS THE LAYER IN WHICH YOU FORMULATE THE MESSAGE CONCISELY.<< Mark de Jong, Kossmann.deJong

>>THE FIRST GLANCE OF AN EXHIBITION IS EXTREMELY IMPORTANT. HOW DO YOU ENSURE THAT UPON ENTERING THE VISITOR THINK: WHERE DID I END UP NOW?<<

Mark de Jong, Kossmann.de Jong

>>DESPITE THAT GREAT DIVERSITY IN STORIES, YOU DO NEED TO CREATE CLARITY. DESIGN HELPS YOU DO THIS.<<

Mark de Jong, Kosmann.dejong

to these. The activation of the concept is the sum of all the foregoing. It now all comes down to concretely activating that which you developed and framed in the other two stages. In doing so, you keep the output from the previous stages on hand and incorporate it in the activation of the concept. We are referring to the following output:

- ESSENCE OF THE VISION
- CORE VALUES
- MOOD BOARD (VISION/VALUES/STORY)
- (CORPORATE) STORY
- FRAMEWORK
- IDEA DIRECTION
- CONCEPT NAME
- DESIGN MAP

6.2.1 ACTIVATION, CONTENT AND DESIGN

For every individual each medium has its own position in between 'knowing' and 'experiencing' on the scale of intrinsic value. The consequence of this is a personal effect, both emotionally and intellectually. In addition, one medium is more powerful than the other. In order to be able to influence this, you can make use of timing. Timing is everything! If you want to activate concept carriers in the right way, you need to carefully think about the moment at which you will do so. When will you launch the communication campaign and when is the right moment for the announcement of your products or service? For a company such as Amazon, for instance, it is useful to start promotions just before the Christmas holidays, because this is the period in which the consumers usually buy presents. In the case of a festival, it is important not to announce the entire programme in one go, but to reveal the line-up in phases. Indeed, this increases the tension of a possible surprise effect. If everything is announced all at once, then the message would not linger as long. Therefore, as a concept thinker you need to very consciously build tension. You constantly ask yourself what you announce when or what content you activate at what moment.

As soon as you have determined the touchpoints and therefore thus the type of content (concept carriers), you will also know what discipline of design you are dealing with. Per touchpoint you analyse all the design layers and on the basis of your design map (the awakening concept), your mood board, and story (dormant concept) you will shape your visceral design. In that way you provide each channel with the right added value. If we circle back to the Gestalt laws, it is important to realise that you apply them in a combination: they enhance and complete each other. Some laws are 'stronger' than others. That is to say, they have a stronger visual impact. Gestalt laws not only apply for visual language, but also ensure the overall experience; all senses work together to process content by means of design. In case of a combination of concept carriers and thus the application of for instance product, environmental and communication design, the Gestalt laws perfectly work to bring your concept to life. A good example of this is Ikea (van den Broek et al, 2010); they make optimal use of the Gestalt laws. For instance, they use the law of similarity: everything is yellow-blue and all locations look alike. The law of continuity is applied by Ikea in the walking routes through the store and the law of proximity is applied through sorting small gadgets and presenting them in the area where they are relevant. For example, the kitchen gadgets can be found in the showroom kitchens at IKEA.

Upon application of design on the content you also take possible layers of stories into account during the activation. These layers now have to be translated into the living concept and become perceptible to the senses. The different story layers of which a concept mainly consists now need to be converted into content and design. As we have already described in chapter 4, it depends on the type of concept whether the story needs to be worked out simultaneously or chronologically. For instance, you can think of an exhibition by a museum or the layout of a theme park: in these examples the layers of the story are offered simultaneously.
The interpretation of the story depends on how the

target group processes it, as described in section 6.1.2. The first glance is highly important in this, particularly for concepts to which the physical environment is an essential carrier. The consumer needs to become receptive to the story upon arrival. You need to enter a space and actually immediately become tempted to dive into the story. The 'first glance' can incite that temptation. It is the primary interpretation of the consumer. They do not immediately have to understand everything, but they should feel something: excitement or entertainment, and it should make them want to know more. You respond to the emotional value of the individual here. Even visitors without any previous knowledge should get the feeling that he or she wants to know more due to that 'first glance'. The consumer with more background knowledge also needs to be triggered to want to get deeper into the story. To this end, transmedia storytelling is a way to allow the consumer to decide how and at what moment he or she will start diving into the deeper layers of the story.
Now that you have a range of information that you need to take into account in the activation of content and design, we want to give you a number of basic rules for the activation of a concept to conclude. Whether it is about product design, design of physical environments, or communication design, the basic rules below will help you to activate design in the right manner:

BALANCE AND HARMONY

This is the balance and the sorting of elements that you have determined in your design map. Coherence and alignment ensure harmony in design. The receiver feel visually attracted to balance and harmony and better understands the message as a result. Terms such as symmetry and asymmetry are important in this. Not everything has to be symmetrical, but symmetry does have calming effect. A symmetrical composition has an imaginary vertical and horizontal axis, which divides left and right into equal parts. Always ensure for a degree of balance in the designs you create. If the balance and harmony in the design are disrupted, the visualisation can appear messy or amateurish. Carefully consider the placement of elements. Consider relevance in this. How important are all the separate elements? What element has to stand out? Ensure that you make optimal use of the space available - your framework. You can play with the elements in terms of size, placement and colour. The more elements you have, the harder it will be to create balance and harmony. Within two-dimensional design a fixed frame, or pattern, can help organise all the elements. Make sure that this frame offers room for multiple applications.

CONTRAST

The moment elements are each other's opposites, contrast emerges. By applying contrast, you can indicate what elements are important: they will stand out in the overall picture. You can do so with colour, shape, typography and lines. If you wish to apply contrast in colour, you can choose colours that are located opposite in the colour wheel. These colours are complementary, such as blue and orange or red and green. Such a combination will attract attention. However, you can also imagine other contrasts, such as warm versus cold, and qualitative contrasts. You can also opt for more balance in the colours by choosing colours that are located next to each other on the colour wheel, such as red and orange. That makes the whole picture more

peaceful. If you opt for this, you will need to work with contrast in a different way, for instance with the use of various shapes and/or fonts.

UNITY AND CONSISTENCY

The concept involves one style. Design makes this visible. People should be able to see what the product or service belongs to by the design alone. It needs to be recognisable due to a coherence between all the elements. This makes the design into one whole. An organisation can make a different poster every year, but the identity of the organisation needs to remain recognisable. Do be careful not to make a mandatory straightjacket; it should not turn into a gap-fill exercise. You need to be able to vary within certain mapped out lines.

EMPHASIS

Some elements need to receive more emphasis than others in order to stand out to the user, especially when your concept responds to expressive values. For text you can do so by making use of various kinds of typography, headings, subheadings, and quotes. You can also work with striking colours or larger shapes.

DETAILS

Attention to detail means that in addition to the overall picture, you also pay attention to the details. As a designer you also need to have an eye for this, as a good design lies in the perfection. Details provide just that bit extra and ensure distinctive capacity and finesse. Details make your design unique.

In sum, you can test the use of design with yourself and/ or the target group(s) on various functions before you start activation. In some cases a question can be easy to answer and in other cases you will need to get out there are enter into dialogue with your target group(s).

REFLECTIVE FUNCTION

DOES THE DESIGN SERVE THE CONTENT, OR VICE VERSA?

IS THE CONTENT UNDERSTANDABLE OR DOES THE DESIGN GET IN THE WAY?

DOES THE DESIGN CREATE NOSTALGIA? DO PEOPLE REMEMBER THE DESIGN?

CAN THE UNDERLYING STORY BE RECOGNISED?

DOES THE DESIGN ENSURE LONG-TERM CONNECTION WITH THE TARGET GROUP?

BEHAVIOURAL FUNCTION

IS THE DESIGN USER-FRIENDLY?

CAN THE RECEIVER FIND THE LOGICAL FOLLOWING ORDER WITHIN THE DESIGN?

DOES THE DESIGN MEET THE NEED OF THE CONSUMER?

IS THE FUNCTION OF THE DESIGN CLEAR?

VISCERAL FUNCTION

DOES DESIGN INCITE TEMPTATION?

DOES THE DESIGN HAVE AN EMOTIONAL IMPACT ON THE TARGET GROUP(S)?

HAVE ALL DETAILS BEEN IMPLEMENTED IN THE FORM?

IS EVERYTHING THAT HAS BEEN USED IN THE DESIGN ACTUALLY NECESSARY? OR CAN THINGS BE LEFT OUT?

DO THINGS THAT ARE PLACED CLOSE TOGETHER ALSO BELONG TOGETHER? IS THERE HARMONY?

IS THERE AN EFFECTIVE CONTINUITY BETWEEN ALL ELEMENTS?

HAVE THE GESTALT LAWS BEEN BROKEN ACCIDENTALLY, OR ON PURPOSE? AND IF THEY WERE BROKEN ON PURPOSE, DO THE ADVANTAGES OUTWEIGH THE DISADVANTAGES?

BUTTS AND SHOULDERS: HOLDING ONTO SYMBOLIC VALUE

'At a certain moment many retailers started asking us whether we could not also make our products in another colour. We did so for the bags. Commercially speaking it was a great success, but it was hardly fulfilling for us personally. It did not feel right. If we do something new, that also needs to be unique. So we cancelled our new line to first get back tot the drawing board. Here we started investigating whether we could add an extra step into the production chain that would do justice to our vision. We believe that holding onto the vision and thus the symbolic value has more commercial value in the long term. Eventually, in ten years' time, we hope to be a brand of which people feel that we have always remained honest to ourselves. Moreover, it helps us to stay on our own course, otherwise you might end up reacting to every stimulus you receive. That will lead to you losing credibility. One of our core values is 'OFFSPRING', as we see our consumers as friends. This is reflected for instance in the shipping of the product, the shoe. We then also send a handwritten letter with it, in which we thank the buyer for the purchase and in which we invite them to keep in contact with us about what they think about the product, for example by sending us photos. We have created our story in making the shoe; now it is up to others to make their own story out of it.'

6.3 CONCEPT MONITORING

The concept has been made perceptible to the senses and is now living. In some cases, we see that the concept is left alone after that and is neglected. In that case, something new is created in the activation of new concept carriers, which does not fit in the overall concept. In this way the concept deteriorates and this harms the meaning of the concept. For various reasons it is not always easy to effectively monitor the concept. For instance, the concept might be quite extensive and complex in nature, that the way in which the concept emerged can make maintenance difficult or that there is a lack of suitable staff to fulfil this function. We often see that the activating party has less of a feel for the design, which causes them to create expressions that are not consistent. Thinking back to chapter 1, in which the activities of the creative industry were named; the development, framing and activation of symbolic value can be organised in various ways. If the activation of the concept takes place within another sector than where the concept was developed, it is harder to effectively monitor the concept. The developer of the concept, often with a background in creative business services, is done after delivery to the client and thereby leaves the responsibility and the monitoring to the activating party. That presents a tricky situation for keeping the concept consistent. Other factors that play a role are of course money, time, and various stakeholders. Therefore, it is desirable that the concept developer maintains an advisory role in the activation of the concept. After all, practice teaches that the original idea is quite quickly deviated from in organisations. Thus ensure that for each choice you need to make in the future you can fall back on the output of the dormant and awakening concept, so that you know which choices support your concept and which do not. Preferably, keep the lines to your developer short. Should the development of the concept be done by an external party, it is advisable to also involve people of the organisation for which the concept is meant in the interdisciplinary team that works on this. This makes it easier for the organisation to 'stick with' the concept. How many people of the organisation are involved and how this occurs depends on the scope and impact of the developed concept on the organisation.

Due to the growth within the creative industry and the insight that multidisciplinary teams and hybrid organisations are becoming increasingly important, we hope to see a future in which every organisation has an in-house concept monitor or developer.

6.4 EFFECT MEASUREMENT

The American economist Richard Caves (2000) once stated that the creative industry has a remarkable character. For one, it functions on the basis of the 'nobody knows principle', which refers to the uncertainty regarding the possible success of the concept. This refers to the living concept, such as films, games and newspapers. There are many factors imaginable that determine the success of a good concept, but to this day it is hard to predict what success in the creative industry is based on.

We believe that the success of the living concept is partly determined by the effective implementation of the dormant and awakening concept. If you effectively go through the process, you at least know what value you wish to create, how you wish to do so, and how this is shaped by means of the right content and design. In many creative subsectors effect measurements are conducted on the basis of predetermined objectives. It is important that there are indicators to monitor. After all, these indicators influence the concept. When we refer to indicators, we mean terms such as brand awareness, image, and brand experience. The determination of indicators is important, as you need to know beforehand what you will be measuring. In addition to these indicators, the facts and figures are important. For example, the sales figures or the number of visitors to a website. The success of an entire concept must be measurable at multiple levels. A concept might be less valuable in economic terms, but extremely valuable for employees of an organisation. You can ask yourself the question of what the concept yields for the economy. And what does it offer the target group and the organisation?

The individual determines in what way the concept is processed and therefore also determines the effect. This refers to the possible effect, the possible emotion, and the possible skills of the experience that the concept might offer the individual. In other words: the manner in which the individual acknowledges and perceives the experience. In the research we conducted, we see that measurement increasingly occurs on the basis of subjective experiences. And that while so many different subjective experiences exist! We wonder whether the type of knowledge an insight that we are looking for here is objectively measurable knowledge at all. Ideas and experiences are subjective realities and therefore call for qualitative research. In addition, these experiences are connected to a specific context. The consumer attributes meaning to experiences and in doing so creates his or her own reality in interaction with the concept or others. This makes it hard to provide a clear overview of the effects of the concept, which is possibly also open to multiple interpretations. During our own investigation it struck us that in America, concepts are activated on the basis of trust: after all, you can hardly estimate what the economic value of the concept will be in advance. By applying 'concept action' subjective experiences and successes emerge and the concepts are then enriched and strengthened on the basis of those. It certainly does remain an interesting matter; the question of whether an increased symbolic value of a concept also leads to an improved economic value. There are organisations, such as Motivaction, that conduct various kinds of measurements in the area of communication and branding research. If you want to know more about communication and branding research, you can also explore terms such as post-testing, facial coding, the Image Contribution Test (IAT) and the Emotional Contribution Test.

With this book we mainly want to activate you to think about the effects you wish to create with your concept in advance. This way, you can take the shaping of your concept into account within the three stages. Sometimes you simply have to start to find out whether something works. In order to get started, we refer you to chapter 7. Here we will offer you tools that you can use. After all, concept thinking is mainly concept action!

INSPIRATION

INSPIRATION

In this inspiration section we provide you with suggestions that can help you truly apply elements from the model of concept thinking. Please be aware that not every suggestion provided here will be equally practical for every type of concept. The starting situation determines how you go through the iterative process of concept thinking. In the various suggestions we distinguish between the dormant, awakening, and living concept and between content and design. We use icons to indicate at what stage you can use the suggestion. These icons refer to the theory in this book. Concept thinking is a process of zooming in and out, the constant back and forth between stages. We simply cannot offer you a clear-cut picture of the concept developer. Every concept developer is different and goes through the development process in their unique manner. As we described in chapter 3, for instance, you might be highly analytical or rather more intuitive. On the basis of these different approaches, elements can also be applied differently. An element can be left out or rather be given more emphasis. The biggest contrast is provided by a comparison between the intuitive method and the analytical method of concept development. By juxtaposing these two extremes, you can assess what appeals most to you. Whereas one person might be more intuitive in nature, the other might be more analytical. Therefore, we opted for limiting our suggestions to a few. We feel that each situation calls for other tools, which means there is no fixed framework to offer. Moreover, what works well for one person, can result in absolute disaster for the next. Thus, you can use this section to gain ideas, obtain insights, and learn about the ways in which you might approach things, but make sure to choose your own route in- and outside of these examples. Adjust and supplement where necessary.

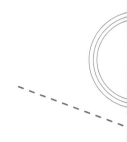

>>DRAW THE ART YOU WANT TO SEE, START THE BUSINESS YOU WANT TO RUN, PLAY THE MUSIC YOU WANT TO HEAR, WRITE THE BOOKS YOU WANT TO READ, BUILD THE PRODUCTS YOU WANT TO USE - DO THE WORK YOU WANT TO SEE DONE.<< Austin Kleon

STAGE:
DORMANT CONCEPT
ELEMENT:
ESSENCE OF THE VISION
SUGGESTION:
I SEE... I FEEL

WHAT IS IT?

'I see... I feel' is a way to formulate your vision. In our method, 'I see... I feel' follows the value fit, which is described in chapter 4 of this book. It is an essential step in the concept thinking method, but also one of the hardest steps.

WHAT DOES IT ACHIEVE?

A vision consists of an objective and a subjective component. The objective component is the factual part, that which you have seen, identified, and investigated. 'I see... I feel' ensures that you start forming an opinion on the basis of the objective information. In other words: this is where you determine meaning at the abstract level for your concept. The choice you make here determines the direction of your symbolic value creation: it forms the basis of further meaning of your concept. It is that with which you will distinguish yourself. Without vision your living concept is the same as that of others', which means you do not stand out.

Let us offer an example of this.

Butts and Shoulders sees:

'We saw all the rigid frameworks in fashion, and with frameworks I mean: you have your seasons, you have your collections, you have your retailers, etc. We wanted to challenge these regular formats. We believe that you ultimately become a puppet of the market if you keep up with the regular formats. You would in principle want to buy a product for the rest of your life.'

Butts and Shoulders feels:

'We believe in slow fashion, and the more you use our products, the more beautiful they will get.' (vision)

HOW DOES IT WORK?

The research part is behind you; now you need to start formulating a vision. The vision consists of two components: 'What do I see?' and 'What is my opinion on that?'. In order to find your answer to these questions, you critically observe your elements. You have already done this in creating the value fit. Should you feel this is a pleasant way of working, you can also refer to your value fit and start 'feeling' something on the basis of that.

Also refer to: Crucq-Toffolo, G. and Knitel, S. (2013). Concept thinking, from dormant to living

IN SHORT, THE FORMULA IS:

WHAT DO YOU SEE (ON THE BASIS OF THE ELEMENTS FROM THE STAGE OF THE DORMANT CONCEPT)?

WHAT IS YOUR OPINION ON THAT?

= THE ESSENCE OF YOUR VISION

Figure 7.1

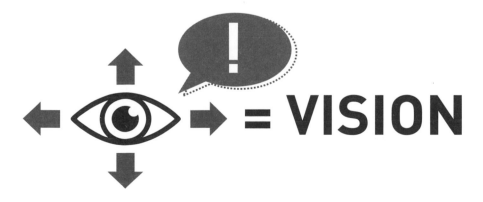

STAGE:
DORMANT CONCEPT
ELEMENT:
CONSUMER ANALYSIS
SUGGESTION:
PERSONA

the target group. Of course, all of this can also be done simultaneously. With all the information you gather, you can then create personas. Usually, you create three or four personas to characterise your target group. Depending on the sector in which your concept is situated, you name certain components. For instance, name, sex, age, place of residence, profession, hobbies, salary, home situation, objectives, motivation, quotes, etc. You can work out all this by means of text and visuals (mood board).

Also refer to:
Run a search on terms such as User Stories, MBTI, and the AIDA model. A stakeholder map can also serve as a basis for creating a persona.

WHAT IS IT?
As described in section 4.1.3, a persona is a non-existent representative, an archetype symbolising a target group. It is an illustration of a target group through both words and visuals. A persona contains certain similarities with the target group and embodies a certain type within your audience.

WHAT DOES IT ACHIEVE?
By making a persona you will better understand your customers and will be able to set priorities more easily. It offers you various perspectives and helps you place yourself in their shoes. It makes something abstract more tangible.

HOW DOES IT WORK?
You can start with a brainstorm session, conducting market research into the existing target group, or interviewing consumers that represent or are related to

STAGE:
DORMANT CONCEPT
ELEMENT:
ORGANISATIONAL
ANALYSIS, AMONG
OTHER THINGS
SUGGESTION:
NARRATIVE INTERVIEWS

WHAT IS IT?

A narrative interview is an interview that yields stories. It is a qualitative, open interviewing method that aims to allow respondents to report largely in their own words and as concretely as possible. This report is about one or multiple events that they have experienced and on the observations, experiences, thoughts, and feelings they had at the time.

WHAT DOES IT ACHIEVE?

Stories are about concrete people, events, and actions. Therefore, stories contain suitable data for determining the initial aspects of social interactions. Here it is merely about descriptions of what happens in reality. These descriptions are viewed in relation to the context. Narrative interviewers therefore do not ask respondents for an objective report; respondents are asked to give an as accurate and concrete account as possible of an event as they have experienced it. That way, an interview can yield new, specific information for the object of investigation and the meanings that people attribute to it.

HOW DOES IT WORK?

The interviewer determines the subject. He or she poses the questions to the respondents and help them in telling stories about their experiences. Thus, it is about the social reality of the respondent. In addition to respect for the conversation partner and an encouraging and open attitude, an effective formulation of the questions is the best way to avoid having your own prejudices confirmed. Effective questions are open-ended, neutral, uncomplicated, and clear. The interviewer can encourage a narrative manner of speaking by asking for a chronological description. The transcripts are interpreted. The goal of this is to determine what respondents say. It is important to pay attention to transitions, and events. Possible criteria for this can be that a change takes place, someone has to make a choice or has made one, or a confrontation occurs between two or multiple actors. On the basis of the interpretation of the transcript lists can be created of for instance words, subjects, themes, people, and theoretical concepts the transcripts refer to. The goal of analysis is gaining insight into the dynamics of meanings in and between stories. The question is how respondents and their stories relate to each other and to the events, actions, and acts they convey. The analysis maps out the differences and similarities between stories, in particular the stories from various respondents about the same events, acts, and actors.

Also refer to:
www.lse.ac.uk/methodology/pdf/QualPapers/Bauer-NARRAT1SS.pdf

STAGE:
DORMANT CONCEPT
ELEMENT:
CONSUMER ANALYSIS
AND ORGANISATION
ANALYSIS
SUGGESTION:
MEANS-END CHAIN
MODEL

WHAT IS IT?

The means-end chain is about determining one or multiple meaning structures. We also call this meaning structure analysis. In a meaning structure connections between values, meanings/consequences, and attributes are outlined. A meaning structure usually contains multiple values, meanings, and attributes. We often unconsciously classify these meanings into an existing structure. The underlying model for this is the means-end chain.

WHAT DOES IT ACHIEVE?

Functional and symbolic values are not separate from each other. It is about the relationship between these values. The model that offers insight into this is the means-end chain model by Gutman (1982). In this model observed product features, the functional and psychosocial consequences of those, and personal values are connected in order to provide an explanation for selection behaviour. In other words: from values to meaning, to that which can be perceived by the senses. Once you have this insight, it can help you to link the right meaning (awakening concept) to the values of the dormant concept. Meaning analysis does not only work through reasoning from product features to ultimate values, but also vice versa. This meaning structure analysis allows you to determine how concrete characteristics of an organisation, service or product can be abstracted to values, and how these values are translated into concrete characteristics.

HOW DOES IT WORK?

By making an inventory of personal values that play an important role within a category or target group, it is possible to translate those to symbolic values and product benefits that are instrumental for those. Those values can then in turn be translated into distinguishing characteristics in the living concept. A means-end chain is generally represented by a value map. In order to draw up a value map it is necessary to interview various stakeholders. The technique that has been developed for this is called laddering. Laddering is based on the 'why' question. For example, a consumer is asked in an interview why he/she considers the answer given important, etc. In this manner you eventually abstract until you arrive at the ultimate values. For further explanation concerning laddering, we refer you to the techniques for laddering.

Also refer to: Rokeach value survey, and techniques for laddering.

Figure 7.2 Means-end Chain Model

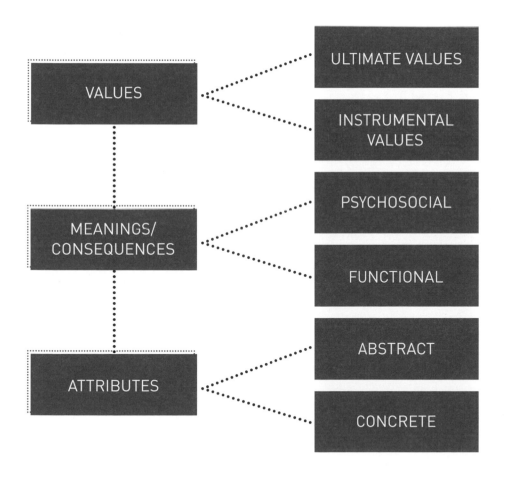

Source: Eurib (2013)

STAGE:
DORMANT CONCEPT
ELEMENT:
ORGANISATIONAL
ANALYSIS AND PROBLEM
EXPLORATION
SUGGESTION:
RICH PICTURE DESIGN
TOOL

WHAT IS IT?

In order to do a problem situation or organisational question justice, you can make use of 'rich pictures'. A rich picture is a kind of visual story that emphasises important experiences or certain aspects. The rich picture is created by someone who is involved in the problem situation and depicts the essence of it as experienced by the person involved. The point of departure is the desire to understand complex, human interactions in a way that is meaningful for all those involved. The rich picture method was originally developed in the field of change management. A rich picture is a holistic representation of the situation with both factual and subjective details.

WHAT DOES IT ACHIEVE?

A rich picture makes it easier to discuss underlying dynamics, which shines a light on the root causes of the situation/problem. It is about the complexity of interaction between people in a certain situation. Making the problem visual often ensures that the problem is put into perspective. Rich pictures can help visualising an experience from multiple points of view (Coenen, 2005).

HOW DOES IT WORK?

The rich picture is created on the basis of interviews with one or multiple stakeholders. During the interview the rich picture is drawn up. The researcher and respondent(s) can jointly draw or allocated this role to either of them. The point of departure in this interview is a clear question. The question is noted at the top of the rich picture. Subsequently, it is investigated what actors (visible or less visible) are of influence on the situation being explored. Cluster actors and attribute symbols to persons or organisations. Arrange these actors in relation to each other and use colours to do so. Finally, supplement the rich picture with qualitative information on actors, such as roles, interests, and/or features. A rich picture consists of three aspects:

STRUCTURE: ACTORS INVOLVED
(ORGANISATIONS AND PEOPLE)

INTERESTS OF THE ACTORS INVOLVED

INTERACTIONS/RELATIONS BETWEEN
THE ACTORS INVOLVED

As soon as the drawing is completed, you can analyse the rich picture. In the phase of analysis it can be useful to make stylized/simplified versions of the rich picture. For instance, you can work with just the main actors, without detailed descriptions, but with an emphasis on the intensity of relationships. During the analysis of rich pictures, the quantitative and the qualitative information is combined. Quantitative information includes for instance the number of factors and the average valuation the respondent attributes to influential relations. While attributing meaning to the qualitative information, the researcher tries to get an idea of the following questions:

WHAT DYNAMICS ARE ESSENTIAL?

WHERE LIES THE CORE?

WHERE LIES THE MAIN CAUSE OF THE PROBLEM?

WHAT STEPS MIGHT LEAD TO A GOOD SOLUTION?

The researcher has an open attitude in this and does not judge. He or she is curious and interested. He or she takes on the role of a person with little knowledge. This allows for new information to emerge every time. Focus is highly important in this: the researcher guards the boundaries of the scope and ensures that all those involved stay within them. After all the questions have been asked, the interview will have resulted in a rich picture and possibly supplementary notes and/or audio recordings. It then makes sense to digitise the rich picture.

Also refer to
www.betterevaluation.org/evaluation-options/richpictures
www.sswm.info/content/rich-pictures

STAGE:
DORMANT CONCEPT/
AWAKENING CONCEPT/
LIVING CONCEPT
ELEMENT:
OUTPUT DORMANT
CONCEPT
SUGGESTION:
MOOD BOARD

WHAT IS IT?

A mood board is a visual overview of images, textures, and colours, possibly supplemented with text, that conveys a certain 'mood' or style. A mood board can be used either two-dimensionally or three-dimensionally with objects in a space.

In the *Immersive world handbook* by Lucas (2013), graphic designer Dave Gottwald provides the following definition of a mood board: "A mood board is a collage of images and other found material done in a large format, such as 24 x 36 inches. It often is flat, but I prefer to employ a more three-dimensional approach. Mood boards are used primarily to gather research and inspiration early on in the creative process and present that material to clients or colleagues."

WHAT DOES IT ACHIEVE?

A mood board is used to visualise the atmosphere or emotion. It provides an overall overview of what you wish to tell and is therefore also a powerful communication instrument. It demonstrates the visual tone of voice, or style. After all, an image sometimes conveys more than a thousand words. You can use a mood board within all stages of a concept, for instance to visualise your target group or organisation or in order to pitch your vision and the accompanying choices to your stakeholders. A visualisation depicts a feeling and directly ensures further dialogue with all stakeholders. In addition, a mood board is a useful aid for a concept developer or designer because it provides direction and inspiration.

HOW DOES IT WORK?

Pose questions to yourself depending the goal of your mood board. What story do I wish to tell? Who is the target group? You can make a mood board on paper, on the computer, or spatially. You can take the images from anywhere: from the Internet, from magazines and of course the photographs you yourself have made. You select images that radiate a certain atmosphere. If you have chosen an atmosphere or multiple atmospheres, you can start with ranking the images and seeing how they fit together. For a three-dimensional mood board you place and rank your objects in relation to each other.

Also refer to:
Scott A. Lukas. (2013), The immersive worlds handbook, designing theme parks and consumer spaces. Burlington: Focal Press.

THE FIRST TRIBE IN

GOODS

HONDA

01234 789

DOMINION
SURVEY
DISTANCE
AND PRECINCT MAP
EBEC

78

WILDFIRE TATTOOS
AT CANADA
Rock·n·Ink

let the
good times
roll

STAGE:
AWAKENING CONCEPT
ELEMENT:
DESIGN MAP
SUGGESTION:
DESIGN MAP

of the concept. For instance, organic or rather more geometrical shapes. The material card offers an overview of all materials that will be used. It is mainly about the ambiance of the materials. Finally, the typography card provides an overview of the fonts that will be used. Typography is always customised work and largely determines the atmosphere of for instance the corporate style or communication medium. All style cards are placed on one large sheet together, offering an overview of the design direction.

Also refer to: Ambrose, G. & Harris, P. (2015). Design Thinking for Visual Communication

WHAT IS IT?
A design map is a visual overview of the design direction of the concept. You could consider the design direction the look & feel of the concept.

WHAT DOES IT ACHIEVE?
A design map displays the overall design. The overall design should form a harmonious whole. The design map indicates whether the overall picture is right and also serves as the point of departure for further designs.

HOW DOES IT WORK?
The design map is completed with style cards. There are four style cards: the colour card, the shape card, the material card and the typography care. For each card you thus make choices and these are illustrated on the card. The colour card displays the colour palette that will be used. For instance, colour families or contrast colours. The shape card displays the visual language

Figure 7.3 Design Map

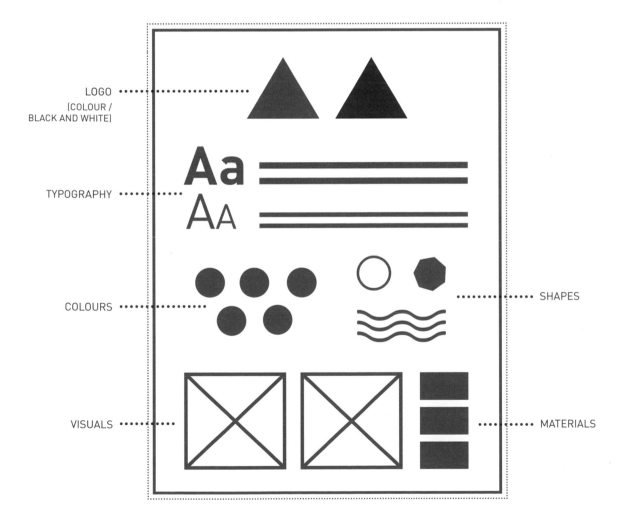

STAGE:
LIVING CONCEPT
ELEMENT:
ACTIVATION OF CONTENT
AND DESIGN
SUGGESTION:
DESIGN METAPHORS

WHAT IS IT?
A metaphor offers a description of an object or idea by comparing it to something else with similar characteristics. You can think of a metaphor as a form of imagery. You use images to trigger and inspire the receiver.

WHAT DOES IT ACHIEVE?
A metaphor brings two different matters together. It is a powerful way to express something. According to Lakoff and Johnson (Metaphors We Live By, 1980) metaphors are even necessary to be able to think conceptually. A metaphor can help you word your feelings. How exactly do metaphors work?

- Metaphors break through boundaries
- They appeal to your sense of imagination
- They evoke recognition
- They make positive associations possible
- They correspond with personal emotions and experiences
- They provide depth to communication
- They reinforce the message
- They anchor values

A good example of thinking in metaphors is the statement by football coach Rinus Michels: 'Football is war.' With this metaphor he illustrates his view of football. Thus you can use metaphors to create new structures. The scientific term for this is synectics.

HOW DOES IT WORK?
In the design process you have a variety of information that serves as the basis for your design. You have a story as your basis. In order to trigger people, you need to shape this information in an effective manner. You can do so with metaphors. There are a number of examples of synectics, according to Roukes (1988), that you can use to get inspired and find the right metaphor. We name a few: personification, comparison, changing scale, combination, replacement, repetition, and isolation.

Using the examples above you can review your concept and think about how you might depict it metaphorically. You can use the world around you as inspiration in order to then make use of one of the aforementioned examples. To get inspired, you could look at film, theatre, politics, architecture, visual arts, books, and history.

Also refer to: Roukes, N. (1988). Design synectics. Stimulating Creativity in Design: Davis Publications VandenBroek.J, Koetsenruijter, W., DeJong, J. & Smit, L. (2010). Beeldtaal: Perspectieven voor makers en gebruikers: Boom onderwijs

>>FOOTBALL IS WAR.<<

STAGE:
LIVING CONCEPT
ELEMENT:
IMPLEMENTATION
SUGGESTION:
CONCEPT TOUCHPOINT
WHEEL

WHAT IS IT?

A concept touchpoint wheel is a framework that makes the touchpoints the consumer encounters transparent. The touchpoints can be tangible (product/service) or non-tangible (service or worth-of-mouth). The frame work consists of the three phases of experience: pre-exposure, exposure, and post-exposure.

WHAT DOES IT ACHIEVE?

The concept touchpoint wheel helps you develop and improve touchpoints. Every touchpoint has an objective and yields value for the consumer. This needs to be taken into account in the design. All touchpoints are building blocks that contribute to the overall experience around an organisation/concept. Every touchpoint thus has a role in the larger whole and completes the experience. An example of this is a clothing store, which has various touchpoints: the display window, the name of the store, the entrance, the retail environment, videos that are projected, the fitting rooms, the counter, the labels on the clothes and much more. The counter needs to display the identity of the brand and needs to be visible: the consumers need to know where they can pay and get information. It needs to be designed in such a way that the consumer can pay in privacy, that there is space for hand luggage and that the products can be wrapped. The role of the counter within the concept touchpoint wheel is that consumers at the counter come into contact with the staff members of the brand. Therefore, it is the human face of the brand. You incorporate the role of your touchpoint and its relation to the entire experience in your design.

HOW DOES IT WORK?

First off, you create a concept touchpoint wheel for the concept. In doing so, you determine which touchpoints are what phase (before, during, or after the actual experience?). You then draw a circle around the touchpoint wheel, in which you indicate what the role of each touchpoint is. In the circle outside that you note down ideas for design choices, fitting in with the overall concept.

Example Scotch & Soda

In order to give you a few more guidelines for filling out the Concept Touchpoint Wheel, we highlight the brand concept of Scotch & Soda as an example. Scotch & Soda is a young Amsterdam concept brand with a love for design and quality. They feel creativity is king and take as their starting point: 'It's about the clothes and nothing but the clothes'. They have a great love for craftsmanship and details. The store of Scotch & Soda radiates creativity and workmanship. In this example, we focus on the touchpoint 'display window'. The role of the display window for Scotch & Soda is that it provides the visualisation of the identity of the brand. It is the first physical encounter with the brand concept. Consumers get an idea of the range and the new products by Scotch & Soda. The overall experience of the brand concept is the most important in this. Scotch & Soda makes various design choices based on its identity and the role of the display window touchpoint. For instance, they have varying themes per season. One of the themes, 'Moroccan Sky', was inspired by the starry sky in Morocco and expressionist art. This theme calls for design choices that fit with both the theme and the brand itself. Scotch & soda divided the display window into three layers (window, garment, and backdrop), for instance designing wooden panels with Arabic visual elements for the backdrop. These visual elements were inspired by Moroccan tiles. The wood hereby represents the craftsmanship that Scotch & Soda wishes to emphasise.

Figure 7.4 Concept Touchpoint Wheel

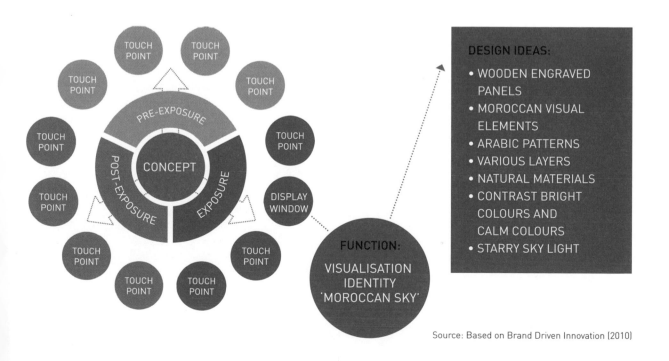

Source: Based on Brand Driven Innovation (2010)

>>ACI WORLD: THE WORLD IS OUR CLASSROOM.<<

Pieter Bon, director of the Academy for Creative Industries (ACI) of Fontys University of Applied Sciences uses the slogan 'I didn't go to school: I went to ACI' to emphasise the aim not to give students the feeling of having gone to school, but having had an experience.

ACI adopts a certain way of thinking about education that highly values both form and content. The concept 'ACI World' views the world as a classroom, considers the city a learning environment, and is convinced that context gives meaning to learning. It is part of the creative industry, changes with its environment, and takes employability as its highest priority. It is all these elements combined that make ACI not merely a school, but a concept.

How is that concept constructed?

ACI WORLD: THE WORLD IS OUR CLASSROOM

Essence of the vision
When you dissect the concept of 'ACI World', you discover three pillars, three convictions that underpin it. The first pillar is about learning: how do people learn? Pieter Bon:

'As and education professional I have always been interested in how people learn, both during my studies and when I became more active in education. One of the things we always ascertained is that we actually do not really know how people learn. In recent years, I have seen that it is important that people can give meaning to learning. That they know why they have to do certain things. Another thing I noticed and still do if for instance contextual learning – and many theories exist on this, too. You can see that people learn when the environment invites them to do so. Space and context are thus important; not just the physical context but in all their elements. You yourself (ed. Sanne Knitel) once indicated that the quality and quantity of your ideas sometimes depend on the space you are in, for instance whether it is red or white. This influences the ideas that you create there. In higher education, where we work for a creative industry, we should actually be in the middle of this, as only that allows students to give meaning to their learning. Only then does that context challenge them to do so, invites them to do so. In the creative industry itself. Education is a type of practice: you do it in an artificial environment or at least in an environment in which you can wonder what real life would actually be like. When we speak of meaningful environments, that is always connected to your learning.'

ACI thus believes that content always needs to be connected to context in order for learning to take place. It is a supporting conviction and, as we will demonstrate, is translated into the concept carriers of the concept.
The second conviction in the concept 'ACI World' is about the objective of learning. What do ACI students learn? Pieter Bon:

'As an academy we say: there are two priorities and they have everything to do with students, namely 'employability' and 'internationalisation'. 'The world is our classroom' is a translation of the idea of 'employability': the capacity to create your own work and income.'

As a concept developer you have an eye for what your client means – even when you are your own client – with values or terms that might contain a specific meaning. Such as in this example of 'employability'. Knowing exactly what a term means is essential for your even-

tual living concept and the way in which you translate this into your concept carriers. If everyone carrying out your concept knows the true meaning, it will be guiding without needing any further explanation and thus contribute to an actually living concept. For instance, to ACI World 'employability' means that all activities are focused on or at least need to contribute to increasing the capacity of students to create their own work and income.

The third conviction of 'ACI World' is directly related to this: the context is international. Pieter Bon:

'(...) we have to be mindful of a generation that has already been with us (ed. the academy) for a number of years and is increasingly oriented towards a changing digital context. We lock these students into a classroom, while digitally they could be all over the world. You cannot hold that attention any longer. You just see it happing right in front of you: the students are occupied with very different things than the lesson. We arrived at the idea to simply extend that context! The context needs to be just as flexible and challenging as the digital world in which they can constantly switch. We also wanted to honour Fontys' vision 'Think bigger'. In ACI's vision 'The World is Our Classroom' the bigger thinking is contained. The thing people might need to get used to is that in addition to thinking bigger, we also really act bigger.'

ACI World looked at and considered the perspective of students, and understands that the world of perception of a student is many times bigger than the classroom. And not only bigger, but also much more accessible and interactive. ACI World wants to make use of that much larger environment, because it recognises that this contains the meaning of learning for the student.

THE EMERGENCE OF ACI WORLD:

THE DORMANT PHASE

Each concept starts with an idea that emerges from a problem or an opportunity. For Pieter Bon, the idea for ACI presented itself in America:

'The first idea for the academy emerged in 2002, when I saw at UCLA (University of California, Los Angeles) that you could make a combination of entertainment and marketing there and that you could actually create degree programmes from those components. World-wide research by PWC (PriceWaterhouseCoopers, ed.) conducted at that moment indicated that many things were about to change in the media and entertainment industry. These developments, in particular the techno-logical developments, would bring about major change in the relationship between producer and consumer, among other things.'

The opportunity Pieter Bon saw in this formed the basis for further exploration and research into trends and developments in the market. In addition to mega trends such as digitalisation and internationalisation, which have greatly influenced the concept of ACI World, ACI discovered a trend that was specifically relevant to it: the application and the making applicable of crea-tive concept development capacity to important social themes such as health care, nutrition, and lifestyle. Pieter Bon:

'(..) we were able to expand to a much broader domain than just 'media and entertainment' and 'event man-agement' or 'gaming': we were able to also work for

>>THE CONTEXT NEEDS TO BE JUST AS FLEXIBLE AND CHALLENGING AS THE DIGITAL WORLD IN WHICH THEY CAN CONSTANTLY SWITCH.<<

>>EDUCATION IS A TYPE OF PRACTICE: YOU DO IT IN AN ARTIFICIAL ENVIRONMENT OR AT LEAST IN AN ENVIRONMENT IN WHICH YOU CAN WONDER WHAT REAL LIFE WOULD ACTUALLY BE LIKE.<<

health care, nutrition, and lifestyle. Beautiful, valuable topics with which we could demonstrate that applied creativity in concept development could also be the order of the day in those domains and sectors. Five years ago concept development and creativity in for instance health care was not at all that common... (...) To my surprise a top sector creative industry was then founded. In that sector it was all about media, entertainment and creative business services. Advertising falls into this, but also design, architecture and events, and even our lifestyle professional is included in the sector. Indeed, I really consider that a creative business services provider who applies his or her creative, conceptual capacity and qualification to provide business advice. In addition, creativity, economy and business advice come together nicely in that. Thus, it is all related to the creative industry, and it has greatly helped that such a top sector emerged. I already knew what category we belonged to, but I had never before heard anyone else define it. Then I thought: I knew it! What we are doing makes complete sense.'

We have seen that in the dormant phase concept developers do not only look at trends, target group and market developments, but also at the existing organisation. How do you apply an idea, the opportunity for which you wish to develop a concept, within your organisation? What core values does the organisation have? Pieter Bon:

'In the past three years, we have defined and described a number of our core values in our policy. Moreover, the programmes do that individually as well. That makes us a ACI again. We have an ambitious, curious culture as an academy (...) As a teacher, I believe you are curious about what happens in that (learning) process. We get students that we deserve, so if we ourselves are not entrepreneurial, curious, inquisitive or mutually attractive, this also influences the students. Research shows that the culture of your organisation – so how your teacher relate to each other – has an incredible influence on and consequences for the success of your students. They feel that, see that, and hear that. In this, leadership is again important. I also feel I personally have an exemplary role in this: it needs to be reflected in the leadership of the organisation. (...) We also wish to have a great societal significance; not just for the city, but also for the region. With that creativity and its application in the sectors of lifestyle, but certainly also in media and entertainment, we wish to add meaning.'

FROM DORMANT TO AWAKENING

In the step from dormant to awakening you connect language to your concept and start concretising your concept. This phase looks deceptively simple, but it is in no way simple. For how do you translate the image, the experience you have of your concept, in such a way that others also experience it? And how do you ensure that that translation keeps being spot on with a continually changing environment around it? Pieter Bon:

'The thing we agreed on with the marketing and communication department from the moment we were an academy is that we show what we do as much as possible. On the basis of that attitude, we started creating our identity and showing who we are. Letting something eventually emerge from that 'action'; it was not a predetermined strategy. (...) That creativity and the application of creativity, learning is creating and creating is learning: at a certain stage we are able to co-sense together and we see teachers (...) take up things of their own accord. To me that represents the power we carry with us; that is exactly the liveliness I try and cultivate.'

Creativity is important during the awakening phase. This is a phase in which you try out and test things and return back to the 'drawing board'. The only defined framework that you have is your vision: that is what you stay loyal to. At ACI World you see that co-creation is an important element in the translation of the vision:

by giving teachers the space to take their initiatives for shaping the concept ACI World, the concept is given a practical dimension. It is also interesting how ACI World ensures that the translation of its vision remains up to date regarding the world around it. Pieter Bon:

'We know that in a changing environment we also need to keep changing. That is why I feel that we have truly made scenario planning a core quality in our research group; it is great to personally apply this to your own academy. After all, you are forced to think in scenarios, to carefully keep an eye out for 'signals of change'. Because you have defined a desired scenario which on the one hand is already what you find yourself in the middle of (...) and thus actually exists, but in which your also have you own wishes – we call them signposts. This allows you to steer that scenario a bit after all. I try to blow some life into it every now and again. In the living concept of ACI World we offer room for things

to emerge. People who see opportunities are given as much space as possible, inside the scope of that scenario with those signposts.'

The way in which ACI World deals with this, beautifully illustrates the iterative character of concept thinking. There is not a single moment at which the concept goes from 'awakening' to 'living': in order to keep your concept alive, you constantly keep an eye on your environment.

FROM AWAKENING OR LIVING

A concept is 'living' when your concept carriers have been shaped, so when the world has met your concept and can experience it. Not just by means of the product or the service you deliver, but also by means of every expression and every touchpoint of your concept. In case of a strong concept the touchpoint supports your vision. How is the vision of ACI World expressed in its concept carriers?

First off, ACI World offers four majors: International Lifestyle Studies (ILS), Communication – International Event, Music & Entertainment Studies (CO-IEMES), Commercial Economics – International Event, Music & Entertainment Studies (CE-IEMES) and Commercial Economics – Digital Business Concepts (CE-DBC). Thus, it provides a versatile course offering for the benefit of the creative industry in the area of media & entertainment and creative business services. The four bachelor programmes are complemented by six minors: Trend watching, Transmedia Storytelling, Game Business, Event, Dance Industry and Design360. For its international students, ACI offers a broad range of Advanced

>>AFTER ALL, YOU ARE FORCED TO THINK IN SCENARIOS, TO CAREFULLY KEEP AN EYE OUT FOR 'SIGNALS OF CHANGE'.<<

Courses. You could consider this the 'architecture' or the 'structure' with which ACI brings its service to the student.

In the coming years, further investments will be made in the ACI Hotspots Tilburg, New York, London, Cape Town and Seoul, in which collaboration on a modern education concept in an urban environment in continued. Every ACI Hotspot will start developing its own Factory and Favourite Meeting Places (FMP's) in which the collaboration with the creative industry and 'serendipity' are a priority. ACI Hotspots are characterised by space for experimentation and being open for the unexpected. Wherever necessary, Houses of Creative Concepts (HoCCs) are designed for the development of entrepreneurship. Every ACI Hotspot has its own 'couleur local', as every city has its own questions.

In addition to Hotspots, Factories, FMPs and HoCCs, ACI World will consist of a broad international network of partner universities and campuses. The emphasis in these developments lies with the organisation and design of place- and time-dependent education.

Media technology will be applied to equip ACI World with the necessary digital support. This includes, for instance, 'remote' assessments, digital testing, digital course offering, and streaming of lessons. More extensive digitalisation should lead to the provision of education and supporting activities increasingly independent from time and place.

>>WE GET STUDENTS THAT WE DESERVE, SO IF WE OURSELVES ARE NOT ENTREPRENRIAL, CURIOUS, INQUISITIVE OR MUTUALLY ATTRACTIVE, THIS ALSO INFLUENCES THE STUDENTS.<<

In addition to this more or less fixed structure of concept carriers, new touchpoints constantly emerge from questions from the environment of ACI World and from initiatives by teachers. Pieter Bon:

'In the past year, we have just found and made the connection with the city here in Tilburg. That city is used as context. The questions from the city come for instance from a local public broadcaster such as Omroep Tilburg, a city marketing lab or a 'City lab', or a festival such as Mundial. In addition, they come from the municipality itself: for instance they want to professionalise their event organisers within the municipality. We have embraced all those questions in the city and used as an environment for students to learn.

An important touchpoint for every concept are the people that carry out the concept, the people with which the consumer comes into contact. This is certainly the case in education, where the teacher essentially delivers the actual 'service' to the student. How does ACI World deal with this? Pieter Bon:

'On the basis of the vision, you hire people and organise the culture to fit. This shapes the personality of ACI, which is also constantly in development and will remain

so. I do not believe the identity is the start. There are always policy plans, management reports, and annually two strategy days. We have also formulated three principles again. ACI will become more of a challenge, which means that we will be leaving that classroom even more. ACI will become ACI World. Those three components are interconnected.

As a team, we need to learn to look every year at where we are, in what scenario we are, and how we will continue. We involve teachers and the IMR (institute's participation council, ed.) in this and this has made us what we are now. That fresh air needs to stay in; we need to continually develop ourselves. The basis is that there is a creative industry that defines creativity according to application in three different ways and that we prepare young people for this. The identity is what it is. We once formulated this in core values. The identity has been formed over the years and will continue to be formed, I think.'

Ultimately, it is about your living concept being an actual experience for people that come into contact with it. That they can experience your concept without having to read your plans. How could ACI World be defined? Pieter Bon:

'If you interpret our ACI World, you would arrive at our students being able to study in another culture in forty places across the world. There are five world cities, including Tilburg (laughs), where we take the questions of that city and the city itself as a learning environment. Not yet to the extent I would like to see that happening, but that is also our world. We have provided 'The World is Our Classroom' with some structure. Admittedly, that is a physical structuring of the world with content elements surrounding and within it, such as the labs (Dance lab, Game lab, Design lab, etc.). We also want to start with a 'Trend lab'. Another interpretation of such an environment is more the 'NY Academy of Creative Industries' and the 'London Academy'. That is a strategic umbrella to indicate that our activities are referred to as such there. Before I get a chance to explain what Fontys is, we will be here for ages; the 'London Academy' is instantly recognised. Further shaping a concept requires constant effort. You need to bring people along in a vision. I hope we will be doing this a lot. We also talk very visually about the academy, instead of using policy language. This gives the academy a certain shape and experience, an image. It is almost philosohical.'

ACKNOWLEDGEMENTS

Writing and the necessary international research leading up to it is people work. Without the time from all the interviewees and without the wonderful facilitating organisation, conducting research would have been a great deal less pleasant. Therefore, our great gratitude to each and every person who directly or indirectly helped realise this book in the past two years. Therefore, we first want to thank our director Pieter Bon and team leader Nick Welman of Fontys Academy for Creative Industries. They gave us their confidence for the second time and believed in our international plans.

We cannot neglect to thank our colleague Bart van Esch, who did the design for our book. Thank you for all the hours, evenings, and phone conversations that we had in order to realise the design of this book. Thank you, it has turned out beautifully!

We also want to thank our colleagues, as they have given us the opportunity in the past two years to regularly be absent in order to work on this book. Special word of thanks goes out to our direct concepting colleagues: Dirk, Ivanca and Chris. Thank you for reading along, thinking along, and your confidence in this method of concept development.

Also our gratitude to Robin Straatman, our student assistant, who has spent drawing up the transcripts. In addition, she is a great writing talent. During the entire process she conducted the final editing. She kept us sharp regarding the writing style and writing conventions. With her critical eye, she was able to make excellent improvements to our story. We feel it has been so special to have been able to offer a student this chance, so Robin, thank you! Regarding the writing process, we finally also want to thank Jacqueline Crucq, who often was approached by us last minute to dot the Ts and cross the Is. She was always prepared to help.

For this book we have been allowed to pick some people's brains for a long time. In our opinion, these people are leaders in the field. They formed a true source of inspiration and continually surprised us with beautiful stories about concept thinking in practice. Thank you Sarah Drummond, Armin David, Robert Doggers, Malika Favre, Lot Frijling, Maryan Brouwer, Gerben Gerritsen, Dirk Hens, Mark de Jong, Niels Jensen, Peter Kentie, Reijer van Kasteren, Michael Kraft, Daniel and Markus Freitag, Daniel Kraft, Aline Ozkan, Ward Monné, Fredrik Öst, Simon Piehl, Anna Snel, Dan Lockton, Karel Willemen and Jan Wilker. A special word of thanks goes out to Fredrik Öst. We asked Fredrik last minute to write our preface. We are very grateful to him that he was able to find time in his busy schedule to do that for us.

Naturally, we also want to thank our publisher at BIS Publishers. Rudolf van Wezel encouraged us to write an international version and thought along with us about the form.
Bionda Dias was always there for any question we had and always gave us honest feedback we were always able to use in order to carry on.

It is the start of April 2016 as I, Gaby, am writing these acknowledgements and I can certainly say that I am grateful to have been able to write this second book. Grateful, but also glad that it is now done. I will not be quick to recommend writing a book while completing your master's degree, working full-time, being a mother of two young children and wanting to be a good wife, friend and family member. These are relatively different activities, in which finding the time can be the biggest challenge. Getting time from my employer for this extraordinary project was therefore a precondition. I am grateful for having had this opportunity to further shape my ambition in this amazing field. I feel blessed that I was able to take all these beautiful trips and was given the time to do so. I feel fortunate with the insights and knowledge I have gained from this.

For an entirely different reason, I also want to take some time to honour my colleague Elaine. Dear Elaine, thank you for all your support in this not always easy process. You were there for me when I needed it the most. Moreover, your eye for design (dizain) has provided valuable input for me.

Someone I certainly may not forget is Marianne. Marianne regularly helped me out when something needed to be translated last minute for the publisher. With my limited feel for language, or rather my lack of feel for language, it was wonderful that I could occasionally draw from your language skills. In addition to drawing from other people's language skills, I was also able to lend Els' ear extensively. Many an evening walk I flooded you with new insights and information. These walks gave me peace and energy to be able to carry on the next day again.

A special word of thanks to my colleagues and friends, Martine and Pieter. Thank you for so much, but especially for not asking how it is going. It is good to know that this is not always necessary to feel supported. The thought that I could always call on you two felt like a gift to me and gave me energy to be able to carry on writing in periods that were tough for me.

This book would not have come into existence without my husband Frank Crucq. Thank you for again having faith and confidence in me. Your wife, who hardly reads any books, just writes them. But especially also the hours in which you naturally took responsibility for the care of our daughters, Sarah and Catoo. My beautiful daughters sometimes did not see me for days due to the travelling I was able to do with great pleasure, and the days that I was stuck behind my laptop and closed off from everything. My family has fully supported me, which is why I want to thank you for your unconditional support.

I, Sanne, would also like to briefly write a few words. How much does a book cost? Not something I would usually ponder for any extended period of time; not a question that you will generally hear me ask. However, becoming the mother of our daughter Jules Mae during the writing of this second book suddenly made that question current and relevant for me. There are choices you weigh, but there are also choices that emerge from unforeseen situations.

It was a challenge to make the right choices and a number of them were hard for me. I made them from the conviction that they were the right ones, but sometimes I felt I did not have sufficient wisdom to be certain of that. The future will tell.

In addition to all the above-mentioned colleagues who have extensively been discussed, I would like to thank my family and friends for their unconditional support and their listening ear. Mum, dad, Rob, Roel, Lenneke, Yvonne and Hans; I am so thankful to you. In particular, I wish to highlight two people who have truly always been there for me (and I truly mean 24/7): my partner Sander and my mother Marleen. Sander is the sweetest, greatest and most caring super-helicopter-viewer I know! We have brainstormed so much together and I was continually bombarded with substantive and critical questions. Sometimes quite annoying, but he definitely continually kept me on my toes. My mother Marleen was truly my rock; the amount of babysitting she took care of as a brand-new grandmother is incredible. Mum, you are amazing!

Finally, I want to thank Gaby, as she continued to carry our book during my leave and did an incredible amount of work. Without her this book would not exist. I am thankful for that.

I hope that all the choices I have made, that everything Gaby and I put into this book, that everything the writing of this book has required from us, will again lead to a valuable contribution to our field, the industry and the education we provide. For that is why we started this. Hopefully it will provide us with a new foundation for continuing in our field and with our development. We hope that you, the reader, have enjoyed reading this book and have found it interesting.

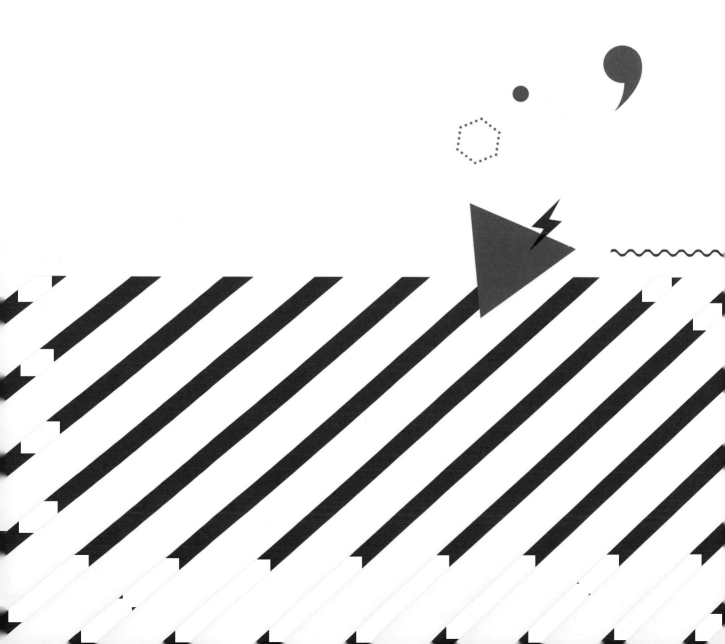

BIBLIOGRAPHY

BIBLIOGRAPHY

Abbing Roscam, E. (2010). **Brand-Driven Innovation. Strategies for development and design:** Ava Publishing

Ambrose, K., & Harris, P. (2015). **Design Thinking for Visual Communication:** Bloomsbury Publishing Plc.

Boswijk, A., & Peelen, E. (2008). **Een nieuwe kijk op de experience economy – Betekenisvolle belevenissen.** Amsterdam: Pearson Education Benelux.

Boswijk, A., Peelen, E. & Olthof, S. (2011). **Economie van Experiences.** Amsterdam: Pearson Education Benelux.

Braams, N., & Urlings, N. (2010). **Creatieve Industrie in Nederland, creatieve bedrijven.** The Hague: Statistics Netherlands.

Van den Broek, J., Koetsenruijter, W., de Jong, J., & Smit, L. (2010). **Beeldtaal, perspectieven voor makers en gebruikers.** The Hague: Boom Lemma Uitgevers.

Statistics Netherlands. (2014). **Monitor Kunstenaars en afgestudeerden aan creatieve opleidingen.** The Hague: Statistics Netherlands.

Coenen, B. (2005). **Humanisering van begeleiding, kritisch-methodische handreikingen voor begeleiding bij complexe organisatie-en veranderingsprocessen.** Soest: Uitgeverij Nelissen.

Csikszentmihalyi, M. (1990). **Flow, the psychology of optimal experience. New** York: HarperCollings books.

Crucq-Toffolo, G., & Knitel, S. (2013). **Conceptdenken. Van slapend naar levend. Basisboek conceptontwikkeling.** Amsterdam: Bis Publishers.

Dale, V. (2014). **Nederlands Woordenboek.** Utrecht: Van Dale Uitgevers.

De Heer, A. (2012). **Content organizing in de praktijk; alles over strategisch inzetten van content:** BIM Media bv.

De Voldere, I., & Rutten, P. (2008). **Cultuur, creatieve industrie en innovatie. Discussiepaper voor de werkconferentie van de Commissie Cultureel Verdrag Vlaanderen – Nederland over creatieve industrie op 26 november 2008:** Van Nelle Fabriek, Rotterdam.

Es, R. (2008), Veranderdiagnose: **De onderstroom van organiseren:** Wolters Kluwer.

Falk, J. H., & Dierking, L. D. (1992). **The museum experience.** Washington D.C.: Whalesback Books.

Flew, T. (2013). **Global Creative Industries:** Polity Press.

Geelhoed, J., Samhoud, S., & Smolders, I.(2012). **Wat is onze naam waard?:** Sdu Uitgevers bv.

Gestalten. (2013), **Brand Spaces, Branded Architecture and the Future of Retail Design.**

Goossens, C. (1992). **Consumptiebelevingsonderzoek in de dienstenmarketing.** Tijdschrift voor Marketing.

Goossens, C. (2000). **Moodmanagement: een overzicht met Marketing-implicaties.** Vrijetijdsstudies.

Guiette, A., Jacobs, S., Loots, E., Schramme, A., & Van den Bempt, K. (2011). **Knowledge partner. Research report. Symbolische Waarde van deCreatieve Industrieën in Vlaanderen:** Flanders DC, Antwerp management school.

Gutman, J. (1982). **A means-end chain model based on consumer categorization processes.** Journal of Marketing, 46(2), 60-72.

Howkins, J. (2001). **The creative economy. How people make money from ideas.** London: Penguin.

Kapferer, J.N. (2003). **Het merk opnieuw uitgevonden.** Deventer: Kluwera.

Kootstra, G.L. (2006), **Designmanagement. Design effectief benutten om ondernemingssucces te creëren:** Peardon, Education Benelux.

Kuiper, G., & Smit, B. (2011). **De imagineer.** Bussum: Uitgeverij Coutinho.

Lee, J. (2013, Feb). TED talk: **Design for all 5 senses.**

Li, C., & Bernhoff, J. (2011). **De impact van social media: van uitdaging naar zakelijk succes.**

Lindstorm, M. (2005). **Brand sense: Build powerful brands through touch, taste, smell, sight and sound.** New York: The free press.

Mccarthy, K., Ondaatje E.H., Zakaras L. & Brooks A.(2004). **Gifts of the Muse. Reframing the Debate About the Benefits of the Arts.** Santa Monica, CA: Rand Corporation.

Michels, W. & Michels, Y. (2011). **Focus op fans.** Zaltbommel: Uitgeverij Thema.

Ministry of Foreign Affairs.(2014). **Made in Holland Creative Industry.** The Hague: Netherlands Enterprise Agency.

Mosmans, A. (2013). **Branding:** Adformatie Groep.

Nijs, D., & Peters, F. (2004). **Imagineering: Het creëren van belevingswerelden.** Amsterdam: Uitgeverij Boom.

Olins,W. (2004). **On brand.** Thames & Amp; Hudson Ltd.

Osterwalder, A., & Pigneur. Y. (2009). **Business Model Generatie.** Deventer: Kluwer

Pine, B. J., & Gilmore, J. H. (1998). **Welcome to the experience economy.** Harvard Business Review.

Press, M., Cooper, R. (2003). **The Design experience: The role of Design and Designers in the Twenty-First Century:** Ashgate Publishing Limited.

Prahalad, C., & Ramaswamy, V. (2004). **Journal of Interactive Marketing.** N.B: Wiley Periodicals, Inc & Direct Marketing Educational Foundation, Inc.

Raaij, W.F. van, Antonides, G. (2002). **Elaboration Likelihood Model.** In: Consumentengedrag; een sociaal-wetenschappelijke benadering. Utrecht: Uitgeverij Lemma.

Schmitt, B. H. (1999). **Experiential marketing; how to get costumers to sense, feel, think, act, relate to your company and brands.** New York: The Free Press.

Stickdorn, M., & Schneider, J. (2010). **This is service design thinking.** Amsterdam: BIS Publishers.

Scott A. Lukas. (2013), **The immersive worlds handbook, designing theme parks and consumer spaces.** Burlington: Focal Press.

Snel, A. (2011). **For the Love of Experience, Changing the Experience Economy discourse,** Oisterwijk: Boxpress.

Stamsnijder, P. (2010). **De vent is een tent: reputatiemanagment in de praktijk:** BIM Media Bv.

Sutmuller, J. (2014). **Serious Concepting. Value through values.** Tilburg: Fontys Academy for Creative Industries.

Rutten, P. (2014). **Kracht van verbeelding. Perspectieven op de creatieve industrie:** Rotterdam University of Applied Sciences.

Roothart, H. & van der Pol, W.(2008). **Van trends naar brands.** Deventer: Kluwer.

Roukes, N. (1988).**Design synectics. Stimulating Creativity in Design:** Davis Publications.

The Work Foundation (2007). **Staying Ahead: The economic performance of the UK's Creative Industries.** Department for culture, media and sport.

Throsby, D. (2010). **The Economics of Cultural Policy:** Cambridge University Press.

Throsby D. (2003). **Determining the Value of Cultural Goods: How Much (of How Little) Does Contingent Valuation Tell Us?** In: Journal of Cultural Economics 27: Kluwer Academic Publishers.

Tongeren, M. (2013). **Een op een, De essentie van retail, branding en design.** Amsterdam: BIS Publishers.

Q&A Research. (2014), **Trendboek retail 2020.**

Throsby D. (2000). **Economic and Cultural Value in the Work of Creative Artists. Values and Heritage Conservation. Research** Report, The Getty Conservation Institute, Los Angeles.

Van Vliet, K. & Wijkhuis, J. (2015). **We moeten eens koffie drinken: over een creatieve industrie die niet bestaat.** Delft: Eburon Academic Publishers.

Van Raaij, W.F., & Antonides, G.(2002). **Elaboration Likelihood Model.** In Consumentengedrag; een sociaal-wetenschappelijke benadering:

Van der Giessen, A.M., Koops, O., Nieuwenhuis, O., & Van Nunen, A. (2015). **Monitor Cross-overs Creatieve Industrie.** TNO 2015 R10132, Final report. Delft: TNO.

Van Gool, W., & Wijngaarden, P. (2005). **Beleving op niveau. Clou.** Uitgeverij Lemma, Utrecht.

Van der Loo, H., Geelhoed, J.,& Samhoud, S.(2008). **Kus de visie wakker:** Academic Service

Wijk, P. (2007). **Corporate storytelling: De marktwaarde van een geloofwaardig verhaal:** Uitgeverij Haystack Zaltbommel.

Zaltman, G. (2003). **How customers think; essential insights into the mind of the market.** Boston: Harvard Business School Press.

INTERVIEWED EXPERTS, VERBAL SOURCE

Drummond, S. (interview), London, November 2015
David, A. (interview), Los Angeles, April 2015
Doggers, R. (interview), Amsterdam, November 2015
Favre, M. (interview), London, November 2015
Freitag, D. (interview), Zürich, January 2016
Frijling, L. & Brouwer, M. (interview), Amsterdam, December 2015
Gerritsen, G. (interview), Amsterdam, March 2016
Hens, D. (interview), Tilburg, March 2016
Jong, M. (interview), Amsterdam, December 2015
Kjærgaard - Jensen, N. (interview), Oslo, 2015
Kasteren, R. (interview), Breda, December 2015
Kentie, P. (interview), Eindhoven, December 2015
Kraft, M. (interview), Rust, May 2014

Kraft, D. (interview), Zürich, January 2016
Lockton, D. (interview), Nieuwaal, March 2016
Monné, W.(interview), Breda, December 2015
Öst, F. (interview), Stockholm, January 2015
Ozkan, A.(interview), Zürich, January 2016
Piehl, S.(interview), London, November 2015
Snel, A.(interview), Amsterdam, June 2014
Willemen, K.(interview), Tilburg, May 2014
Wilker, J.(interview), New York, April 2015

WEBSITES (LAST VISITED: APRIL 2016)

http://www.creatieveindustrieinbeeld.nl/
http://www.shoppermarketingupdate.nl/een-brandstore-voedt-je-verhaal/
http://customerfirst.nl/blogs/2015/01/6-stappen-voor-het-bouwen-van-een-customer-journey-map/index.xml
http://www.acceptemail.com/nl/blog/de-invloed-van-customer-touchpoints-op-de-klantbeleving
http://www.mycustomer.com/experience/engagement/mapping-your-customer-journeys-across-touchpoints-examples-and-techniques
http://www.emerce.nl/achtergrond/positieve-merkervaring-optimalisatie-touchpoints
http://www.storytellingmatters.nl/corporate-branding/item/waar-vinden-storytelling-contentmarketing-en-inboundmarketing-elkaar.html
http://www.frankwatching.com/archive/2009/06/15/transmedia-storytelling-trend-of-tool/
http://www.tedxeutropolis.eu/
http://www.instituutvoorbeeldtaal.nl/
http://topsectoren.nl/creatieve-industrie
http://www.ideate.nl/design-thinking/

https://www.tno.nl/nl/over-tno/nieuws/2015/3/wat-kunnen-andere-sectoren-leren-van-de-creatieve-industrie/

http://vandeinhoud.nl/content-marketing/wat-is-content-marketing

http://harmbalvers.com/2013/09/24/inside-out-versus-outside-in/

http://www.creatieveindustrieinbeeld.nl/

http://resources.goanimate.com/marketing/what-is-a-storyboard-and-why-do-you-need-one

http://resources.goanimate.com/marketing/what-is-a-storyboard-and-why-do-you-need-one

http://accad.osu.edu/womenandtech/Storyboard%20Resource/

https://vimeo.com/blog/post/storyboarding-basics

http://www.businessdesigntools.com/2011/12/storyboards/

http://www.lse.ac.uk/methodology/pdf/QualPapers/Bauer-NARRAT1SS.pdf

dspace.library.uu.nl/bitstream/1874/23553/5/c4.pdf

http://www.servicedesigntools.org/tools/8

https://canvanizer.com/new/customer-journey-canvas

http://www.designthinkersacademy.com/freedownload_customerjourneycanvas/

http://www.cmodigitalforum.com/2016/01/08/need-know-customer-journey-mapping/

http://www.i-scoop.eu/customer-experience/customer-experience-beyond-customer-journey-mapping/

Pretotyping.org

http://knowwithoutborders.org/unpacking-design-thinking-prototype/

http://www.innovationexcellence.com/blog/2015/10/19/how-design-thinking-uses-story-and-prototyping/

http://www.gomoodboard.com/

http://www.creativebloq.com/graphic-design/mood-boards-812470

https://itunes.apple.com/en/app/moodboard/id355893506?mt=8

http://www.instituutvoorbeeldtaal.nl/evenement/visuele-metaforen-13-februari-2014/

http://www.cc.gatech.edu/classes/AY2013/cs7601_spring/papers/Lakoff_Johnson.pdf

http://www.leeds.ac.uk/comms/tov/tone_of_voice.pdf

http://www.degoedegastvrouw.nl/blog/verbeter-je-klantervaring-maak-een-touch-point-analyse/

http://www.customerjourney.nl/home/visie/

http://www.elisamedia.nl/file/98/EM_Introductie_InteractionDesign.pdf

http://www.ics.uci.edu/~wscacchi/Software-Process/Readings/RichPicture.pdf

http://www.samenspraakadvies.nl/publicaties/Handout%20scenario-ontwikkeling.pdf

ILLUSTRATION CREDITS

Page 50: Noë Flum
Page 51 (top center): Bruno Alder
Page 51 (bottom right): Noë Flum
Page 52: Noë Flum
Page 53, 54, 55: Roland Tännler
Page 56, 57: www.flufif.com, Fabian Scheffold
Page 59, 60: Rapha
Page 103: www.buttsandshoulders.com
Page 104,105: www.thisisus.nl, Pim Welvaarts
Page 112: www.mikenicolaassen.nl, Mike Nicolaassen
Page 125: www.buttsandshoulders.com
Page 135: Jimmy Eriksson
Page 136, 137, 138, 139: SNASK
Page 147: www.thisisus.nl, Pim Welvaarts
Page 167: www.flickr.com
Page 170, 171, 173, 174, 175 (bottom left), 177,
        178, 181: Academy for Creative Industries
Page 175 (bottom right): Christianne Heselmans

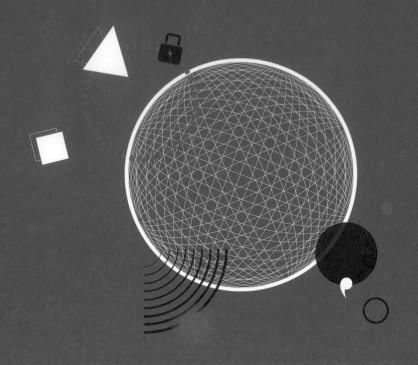